Praise for *Marketing in the Age of Google*

"Vanessa Fox is not only blessed with a brilliant mind, but fantastic perspective into the search marketplace. Her experiences at Google and within the industry, combined with her ability to share those insights in easy to understand morsels makes this book a must read for anyone with even the slightest interest in what's happening in the online world."

—Richard Zwicky, Founder, Enquisite

"Vanessa Fox grabs your hand, shows you the way into the big black box of search marketing, and flips the lights on. Trying to justify a search-related project? From hard data to helpful checklists, it's all in here. Taking on the challenge of search optimization by yourself? You'll walk away from this book not only *getting* it when it comes to using search to build your business, but knowing how to *do* it."

—Tamara Adlin, cofounder of Fell Swoop and
author of *The Essential Persona Lifecycle:
Your Guide to Building and Using Personas*

"Finally! A C-level book about smarter search engine marketing. *Marketing in the Age of Google* by Vanessa Fox is undoubtedly the search marketing bible for senior executives looking to maximize business growth through search engine marketing. This is a must read and if you don't, your competition certainly will."

—Lee Odden, CEO, TopRank Online Marketing

"Former Googler Vanessa Fox has a unique understanding of search marketing from both sides of the table and has been educating people about the wonderful world of Google and search marketing through speaking and writing for years. Now she compiles all her great knowledge in book form and thoughtfully guides newcomers and the experienced alike past jargon and distractions to focus on the best ways to achieve success in today's searching culture."

—Danny Sullivan, Editor and Chief, Search Engine Land

"This tome may be the first book that manages to identify and deconstruct the new search-engine-centric world in which we live. With insights and tips for anyone doing business in the connected world, it's perhaps the first must-read-to-survive business book of the twenty-first century. Highly recommended."

—John C. Dvorak, columnist Dow-Jones Marketwatch, *PC* Magazine

"Let's face it—in today's online world, marketing is technology, and the hottest technology is search. No one knows the business of search engine optimization better than Vanessa Fox. The lessons in this book provide a strategic framework to understand how search has forever shifted consumer behavior and how businesses can adapt to thrive in the era of search."

—Conrad Saam, Vice President of Marketing, Avvo

"Vanessa is the rare person with big picture expertise who has spent time deep in the trenches with sleeves rolled up making the magic happen. This book reflects that on every page. Get ready to finally stop marketing on the web as if it were television!"

—Avinash Kaushik,
Google Analytics Evangelist
Author of *Web Analytics 2.0: The Art of Online Accountability and
Science of Customer Centricity*

"If you are an entrepreneur, webmaster, designer, or an executive for a Fortune 500 company, *Marketing in the Age of Google* will help you streamline your business strategy based on understanding your customer. I would recommend it as reading material to every project manager within eBay."

—Dennis Goedegebuure, Senior SEO Manager, eBay

learn how to bring search engine optimization (SEO) out of the black box and into the creative, collaborative, process that has driven smart advertising for decades. This is a necessary addition to all of our reading. "

—Jorie Waterman, Senior Vice President and
Director of Search, MRM Worldwide

"Eighty-five percent of the clicks on Google's search engine happen in non-paid results. This book analyzes and explains the rapidly changing landscape of those results, and shows you how to leverage them for business. It's an informed and essential contribution to the field."

—Adam Audette, President, AudetteMedia Inc., and Lead SEO for Zappos.com

"Why is a Bing guy giving a quote to a book with Google in the title? Because Vanessa does two things: nails the core truth behind how consumers are using engines today (it's not what you think!) and gives you *actionable* things you can do *today* with free tools to help convert searchers into customers. Finally, a book that combines theory and practice without making me feel like I'm the dumbest guy in the room. Also, Vanessa's impressive citing of quotes from other people and the use of my data (check out Chapters 2 and 3—they are epic) make this book not only believable and an indispensible tool to impress your boss, but a great conversation starter at search conference parties. Believe me, you need it."

—Stefan Weitz, Director, Bing Search

"Fox elegantly explains how search is an essential component of any business' marketing strategy. Her comprehensive statistics should convince even the most skeptical of the need to invest in search."

—Jonathan Hochman, Hochman Consultants

"I have long considered Vanessa Fox the go-to expert on search . . . for everyone from individual publishers to big brands. With her new book *Marketing in the Age of Google*, she's finally doing us all a great service and putting all of that knowledge and strategic insight into one easily digestible place."

—Elisa Camahort Page, Cofounder and COO, BlogHer

"These days, there's a wealth of information available that teaches the techniques necessary to achieve top rankings in search engine results or paid search listings. But few books go beyond tactics to show you how to truly engage with your customers through search and building meaningful relationships that lead not just to results, but to relationships that can last a lifetime. *Marketing in the Age of Google* does just that, making it a unique and invaluable guide to the full spectrum of activities and touch points that are the hallmarks of truly successful search marketing campaigns."

—Chris Sherman, Executive Editor, SearchEngineLand.com, and
President, Searchwise

"I devoured this well-written and very organized book, and quickly determined that this information is a game-changer for most companies. Senior management and corporate America no longer have excuses for not understanding search and SEO. Vanessa explains complex search concepts using easy-to-read, real-world examples. Only she could have written this definitive SEO reference manual. This is the type of book that even the most experienced search professional will return to again and again. Whether you are an executive, newbie or experienced corporate SEO, this book is required reading. I found myself thinking about these search tactics long after I put down the book. Every reader of this book is receiving the highest-level SEO consulting with every turn of the page."

—Rudy De La Garza, Jr., SEO for Bankrate.com, and Owner, SEOMarketing.com

"Vanessa Fox brings a delightful and insightful approach together to help business owners understand the key tenants of marketing in today's online world of metrics and search—and more important, gives clear guidance on what they need to do to be successful. This book is a must have for every CEO and marketer."

—Natala Menezes

"One of the most in depth, clear reviews of the essence of search marketing and its influence on modern business. Well-balanced in its approach and examples, this book is chock full of insights from the brightest minds in search marketing today. From explanations of how we got to where we are, to clarifying future directions business owners should watch, *Marketing in the Age of Google* should be included as part of any businesses plan for success on the Internet."

—Duane Forrester, Sr. Program Manager (SEO), Microsoft

"This is a *great* book. I want to recommend it to every client who's ever asked me for search strategy advice! *Marketing in the Age of Google* provides invaluable information about techniques and tools you can use to improve your organic and paid search results — but more importantly, it explains why your customers' needs, desires, and behaviors should be the central focus of your search marketing strategy. Also, "Would You Like to Exchange Links with My Site Buy-Cheap-Viagra-While-You-Play-Poker-Online-and-File-a-Mesothelioma-Class-Action-lawsuit.info?" is the best heading ever."

—Debby Levinson, Founder, Nimble Partners

"Search, aim, market. If you want to increase your sales without doubling your sales force, read on. Vanessa Fox opens up the hood of leading search engines and gives us a very insightful tour. Every business manager should know how search works to stay competitive. At the end of the day, running a business without an online strategy is like sending all your online customers to your competitor—you missed the sale because you did not show up."

—Melek Pulatkonak, President and COO, hakia.com

"Vanessa takes what is certainly the most important marketing topic of the decade, and makes it not only accessible but concrete. A must read for marketers; it rises above a mere playbook of tricks and tips to showcase the principles of successful marketing with and through search."

—Randall Lucas, Venture Capitalist, Voyager Capital

"It's hard to succeed on the Internet without understanding the mechanics of search marketing and the technology behind it. Vanessa's book breaks down key technological and marketing elements in a way that's easy to understand and apply regardless of your level of marketing or IT expertise. Do you want more visitors to your Web site? Do you want to be known as an authority online? If yes, this book will help you understand and take advantage of the marketing opportunities behind search technology. It's a must read."

—Debra Mastaler, Founder, Alliance-Link

"Vanessa Fox has delivered great search marketing insights with her new book *Marketing in the Age of Google*. She has successfully translated the complex search marketing concepts into easy to understand ideas that can be implemented by everyday business owners who do not have a PhD in computer science."

—Greg Niland, GoodROI

Marketing

in the Age of

Google

YOUR ONLINE STRATEGY *IS* YOUR
BUSINESS STRATEGY

VANESSA FOX

WILEY

John Wiley & Sons, Inc.

Published by John Wiley & Sons, Inc., Hoboken, New Jersey.
Published simultaneously in Canada.

For general information on our other products and services or for technical support, please contact our Customer Care Department within the United States at (800) 762-2974, outside the United States at (317) 572-3993 or fax (317) 572-4002.

Wiley also publishes its books in a variety of electronic formats. Some content that appears in print may not be available in electronic books. For more information about Wiley products, visit our Web site at www.wiley.com.

Library of Congress Cataloging-in-Publication Data:
  Fox, Vanessa, 1972-
  Marketing in the age of Google: a non-technical guide to search engine strategy / Vanessa Fox.
    p. cm.
  Includes bibliographical references and index.
  ISBN 978-0-470-53719-0 (cloth)
  1. Internet marketing. 2. Internet searching. 3. Web search engines. I. Title.
  HF5415.1265.F678 2010
  658.8'72—dc22

                                                                2009047256

Printed in the United States of America.

10 9 8 7 6 5 4 3

To the search marketing community:
You have been welcoming beyond description
since the very beginning. This book
wouldn't exist without you.

Contents

Foreword

There's a special place where customers gather each day, willingly seeking businesses that can help them. They want cars. They want plumbers. They want music downloads. They want vacation rentals, lawn care products, tax advice and more. You name the product or service, this place has someone looking for it.

This venue is the ultimate destination for those after a prequalified audience. Everyone there is ready to buy or convert in some way. Everyone is explicitly asking to be contacted. Everyone is even willing to take part in market research to help guide a business forward. Here's the best part: As a business, it costs nothing to be admitted.

What's the catch? There isn't one, other than being aware of the opportunity this place provides and tapping into it.

The place? The major search engines used by millions each day. Yahoo!, Microsoft's Bing, and the largest of them all, Google. Consumers increasingly depend on these tools to locate products, services and information. Search engines continue to usurp more "traditional" means of reaching customers, such as newspapers, phone books, or television. But unlike those traditional means, getting in front of consumers through search engines doesn't require a huge marketing budget.

Search engines mine web pages and other digital content to automatically provide answers to those searching. Becoming one of those answers can require no work at all. Many companies just naturally turn up in the search listings—for free.

With a little savvy, companies can increase their representation. Have you thought about the exact ways people might be searching for your goods? Have you ensured that search engines can properly read your Web site? Have you considered how you're listed beyond your Web pages, in areas such as video results?

The hardest part of success with search engines isn't the tactical changes or techniques involved. It's simply becoming "search aware" in the first place—of understanding the importance of search and ensuring that you're not ignoring easy-to-take opportunities or establishing barriers that block your potential.

That's where this book comes in. It will help you over that hardest part: gaining search awareness. In it, Vanessa Fox illustrates the importance of search for today's marketer. She breaks down search marketing into common sense components that won't make you feel lost in jargon or tactics.

I've written about search marketing for nearly 15 years now, and it still amazes me that more people still don't understand the incredible value it holds. Discover the importance of search in this book, how it can help you reach your customers and discover new directions to take your business. Read on about the new age in marketing—that of Google and search engines.

—Danny Sullivan, Editor-in-Chief,
SearchEngineLand.com

Preface

When I worked at Google, I talked to thousands of business owners seeking my help and advice. To them, Google was somewhat of a black box. They knew that organic search (the unpaid result set) was important, but they had no idea how to use search data and customer acquisition from organic search in their business processes.

We built Google Webmaster Central[1] as a way to give business owners and Webmasters insight into how their sites were performing in Google and to help them identify problems and make improvements. During my tenure at Google and since, the business owners I talk to often fall into one of the following camps:

- Those who know search has become an important part of the customer engagement cycle, but aren't sure where to start.
- Those who don't think search is that important and believe that even if it is, businesses shouldn't have to concern themselves with it. It's Google's job to sort things out.
- Those who get so caught up in optimizing their sites and ranking number one that they don't step back to look at the bigger picture: to understand how searchers behave, how to engage with them, and how to turn them into lifelong customers.

After I left Google, I wanted to take what we started with Webmaster Central and go beyond helping people pinpoint issues that might be preventing them from doing well in search. I wanted to help them fix those areas, improve their sites, and take the focus *off* of ranking and put it *on* connecting with the right audience. In short, I wanted to change the conversation about search. I wanted to help businesses understand why organic search was important to their long-term success and show them how to harness it for better customer engagement, more informed business and product strategy—and introduce them to a whole new world of customers who they may have been missing. Thus, the idea for this book was born.

If you've picked up this book, you already realize that search is becoming the primary way in which many people get information, decide what to buy, and make those purchases. And you know that as customer behavior changes, businesses remain successful by changing with them.

These days, your search strategy *is* your business strategy, whether you realize it or not, because that's how potential customers are trying to find you. Search is the new Yellow Pages, 800-number, Sunday circular, card catalog, and cash register.

But how do you build a comprehensive search strategy? And how can you take advantage of the amazing amounts of data that search makes available about your potential customers? Much as our evolution to a searching culture was a fundamental shift in behavior, fully realizing the potential of search often requires such a shift in your business. This adjustment will help you better connect with potential customers, make more informed business decisions, and remain relevant as our world continues to change. This book will get you there.

CHAPTER

How Search Has Changed Your Business

Twenty years ago, the World Wide Web as we know it today didn't exist. Ten years ago, only early technology adopters used search engines, and Google was a struggling young upstart. Now, over 50 percent of online Americans use search engines every day and over 90 percent of them use search engines every month. That's a lot of potential customers who are looking for you and a lot of market research about what those customers want.

Americans conduct 22.7 billion online searches a month[1] and worldwide, we type into a search box monthly 131 billion times. That's 29 million searches per minute.[2] It's safe to say that we've become a searching culture. Just take a look at the 2009 Super Bowl to see this in action. Look at the spiking searches on Google the morning of the big game. Thirty-five of the top 100 have the word "Super Bowl" in them, and another 27 are Super Bowl–related (see Figure 1.1).[3]

Business leaders know that the world is changing. More customer research and transactions take place online now than ever before, and those numbers are only going to increase. Globally, the number of searches grew 46 percent in 2009. According to Jack Flanagan, comScore executive vice president, "Search is clearly becoming a more ubiquitous behavior among Internet users that drives navigation not only directly from search engines but also within sites and across networks.

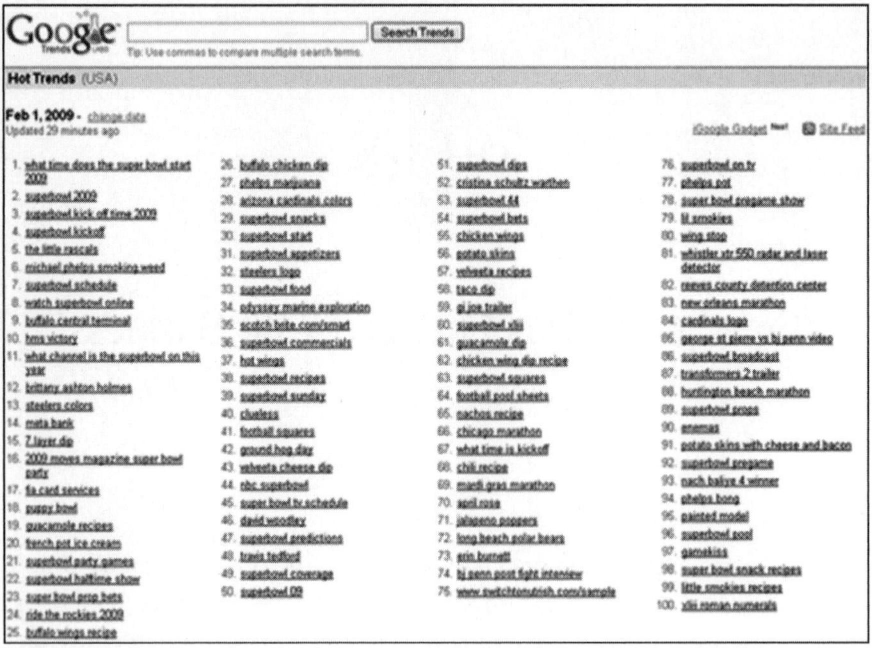

Figure 1.1   Google Search Trends, Super Bowl 2009
Source: Google Trends

If you equate the advancement of search with the ability of humans to cultivate information, then the world is rapidly becoming a more knowledgeable ecosystem."[4] But many professionals simply aren't sure how to evolve their businesses to best take advantage of this changing landscape. This book will show you how to think about your business in a new way, to better connect with your customers through search, and to weave the value that search provides into all aspects of your organization.

Through organic search, you can reach potential customers at the very moment they are considering a purchase and provide them information exactly when they are looking for it. While many businesses are attempting to connect with their potential customers through paid search (such as with Google AdWords), the opportunity to reach these customers through organic search—the results that are algorithmically generated rather than paid for—remains largely untapped. In fact, 88 percent of online search dollars are spent on paid results, even though 85 percent of searchers click on organic results.[5] Search is a fairly unique opportunity to connect with your potential customers.

Never before have we had access to such remarkable amounts of data about potential customers. We know what they search for (and what they don't). We know how they shop and how they buy. We can even find out where they look on a page. Businesses spend such significant amounts of time and money on market research, focus groups, and usability studies, yet so many fail to augment this information with the abundance of free data available from those 113 billion searches a month.

We don't have to look farther than our local newspapers to see how consumer behavior has changed. The newspaper industry spent years trying to get readers to return to their old behaviors of expecting the newspaper at their doors every morning, and reading the stories as they were laid out in print. But those readers had moved on to searching online for news on topics of interest and getting that information in real time rather than a day late. Similarly, companies have to adapt and evolve with their customers instead of attempting to get their customers to return to their old ways.

Doesn't Google Show the Most Relevant Sites to Searchers *Without* My Input?

I was recently talking to *Wired* magazine senior writer Steven Levy (previously the senior technology editor for *Newsweek*), who's been spending a lot of time at Google researching his book, *Searching for Google*.[6] Levy doesn't believe that businesses should have to do anything "special" to their sites for Google since Google's purpose is to surface the most relevant, useful results to the top. He compares the practice of site owners trying to influence this to students having coaches for the SAT exam.

I told him I didn't see things that way at all. I see the situation as similar to a retailer who opens a store in a new city. Before leasing a building, they'll likely scout out the area to find the best corner. They'll do some competitive research to see where the other retailers are located, as well as some customer research to see where their target consumers shop. (Many even stand on sidewalks and count people walking by!) Retailers know that even if their store has the most amazing merchandise at super low prices, they might not have many customers if they open their store in an alley that's closed to traffic and they don't let anyone know they're there. John Deere probably wouldn't have many people buying riding lawn mowers in a store in Manhattan.

Companies should think of their online presence as another "retail location." Organic search is the city they're in, the street they're on, the sign above their door. John Deere opens stores in towns where people have really big lawns, and they keep the doors unlocked so their customers can get in. If you don't do the same with organic search, you're missing an increasingly large percentage of your potential customers.

The Keys to an Effective Search Strategy

To incorporate search into your organization:

- Add search metrics to your data mix to better understand your audience, see industry trends, and build a better product strategy.
- Integrate offline and online marketing activities to capitalize on your offline advertising efforts and to keep from losing potential customers that your offline advertising efforts are driving to search engines.
- Develop a search acquisition strategy that fully harnesses the searching behavior of your potential customers.

To successfully execute your search strategy, you should build its importance into every aspect of the organization—not just marketing. A successful search strategy depends on IT and Engineering, Product Marketing, Business Development, Marketing and Advertising, PR, Customer Support, User Research, User Interaction Design, and any other department that thinks about the business, customers, product, or Web site. *Marketing in the Age of Google* will guide you toward building a successful search strategy and extending the process for execution throughout your entire organization.

This book talks about organic search—the search results that are generated algorithmically based on what the search engines think is most relevant for the query. Paid search (the ads that appear beside the organic results) is also an important piece of the search strategy puzzle but a number of resources exist to help businesses better understand and use paid search so in this book we'll only be talking about it as it influences organic search.

What is your organic search strategy? If you don't have one, you're missing a key piece of your business strategy—and shutting out many potential customers who are looking for your business. If you're an executive, this book will give you a holistic view of how search fits into your overall business strategy and how to integrate it into the organization. If you're a marketer, developer, user interaction designer, or otherwise work on customer engagement, product development, or company awareness, this book will show you how to incorporate search into what you're already doing for an even better return.

Search as the Entry Point of the Web

For many of us the search box has become our entry point to the Web. When the Web first gained popularity, it became important for a business to have a Web site. As online activity became more prevalent, it became important for a business to include a domain name in advertising and other materials. Now things have shifted again, and it's vital for a business to rank well in search results both for their brand name and for queries relevant to the business.

But integrating offline and online marketing is only half the story. It's just as important to understand the needs of your customers. For years, companies have commissioned focus groups and large-scale surveys and conducted massive market research to find out what their potential customers want and how their current customers think about them. All of those activities are still valuable, but there's now an easier (and cheaper) way. Search can provide powerful data about exactly what your potential customers want and what they're thinking about you.

Every Day, Millions of Potential Customers Are Telling You Exactly What They Want

Intuit sells accounting software. Their product packaging, marketing materials, and Web site all refer to this software as *bookkeeping*

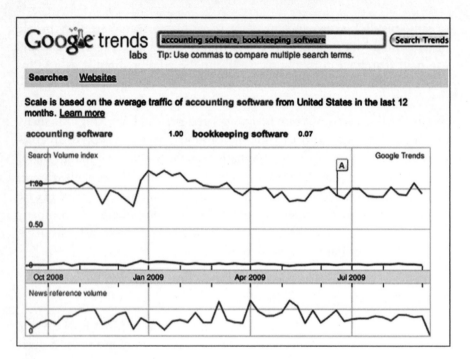

Figure 1.2   [Accounting] and [Bookkeeping] Search Volume
Source: Google Trends

applications. But if you take a look at what their potential customers are searching for, you'll notice that it's "accounting" over "bookkeeping" software by a substantial margin. (You'll learn how to find out how your customers are searching for you in Chapter 2.) See Figures 1.2 and 1.3.

Not only is Intuit missing this audience from its search acquisition funnel, it's not resonating with its potential customers as well as it could be in offline channels.

The National Institutes of Health (NIH) has an important mission to make accurate and useful health-related information available to the American public but limited resources with which to do so. If this group wants to help the greatest number of people first, it could start with search data. You can see below that many more people are looking for information on arthritis than on heart disease. See Figure 1.4.

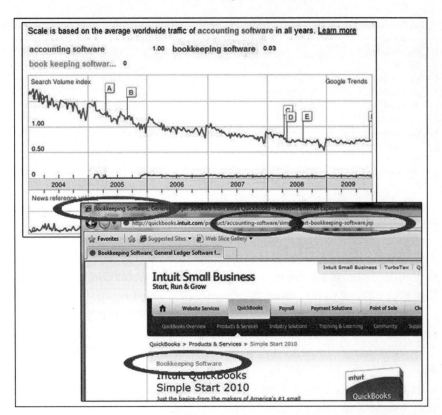

Figure 1.3 Speaking the Language of Your Customer

Source: Google Trends and Quickbooks.Intuit.Com

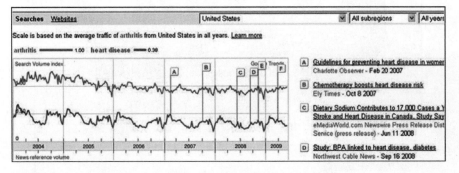

Figure 1.4 [Arthritis] and [Heart Disease] Search Trends

Source: Google Insights for Search

Search terms related to arthritis				
Top searches		⑦	**Rising searches**	
1. rheumatoid arthritis	━━━━━━━ 100		1. what is arthritis	Breakout
2. arthitis pain	━━━━ 55		2. symptoms of arthitis	Breakout
3. arthitis symptoms	━━ 30		3. hip arthitis	Breakout
4. arthitis treatment	━ 25		4. back arthitis	Breakout
5. arthitis knee	━ 25		5. arthitis pain	+180%
6. arthitis foundation	━ 25		6. arthitis treatment	+120%
7. what is arthitis	━ 15		7. arthitis knee	+80%
8. symptoms of arthitis	━ 15		8. arthitis foundation	+80%
9. back arthitis	━ 15		9. arthitis symptoms	+70%
New! ▸ Google			10. rheumatoid arthitis	+60%

Figure 1.5   [Arthritis] Search Trends
Source: Google Insights for Search

Diving deeper, we can see that "rheumatoid" is the type of arthritis that people search for the most and that Ohio's population has one of the keenest interests in this topic. See Figures 1.5 and 1.6.

Many factors go into prioritizing projects, but your potential audience's primary interest can be a valuable one.

Whether you run an online business, a multinational conglomerate with no online presence, or a two-person startup out of your garage, your customers are providing you with valuable data that can help form your business strategy.

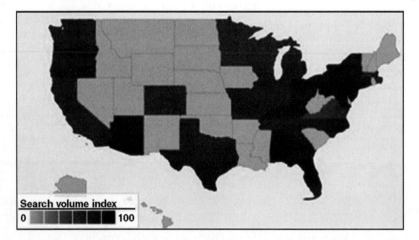

Figure 1.6   [Arthritis] Regional Search Trends
Source: Google Insights for Search

How Search Has Changed Marketing

As defined by the Chartered Institute of Marketing, marketing consists of "identifying, anticipating and satisfying customer requirements profitably."[7] That definition doesn't change as business moves online.

But while the core elements of marketing remain the same, it's no secret that consumer behavior is shifting. We frequently turn to online sources for things we used to get offline—from news and local directories to television shows, music, and movies. This evolution means that the expectations of your potential customers and their methods of interacting with you may be different than before. For instance, they may expect support online, whereas before they may have looked for an 800-number.

This shift also means that traditional forms of advertising don't have the reach that they used to have. If 10 million fewer people are reading the printed newspaper in April, 2009 than April, 2008,[8] then 10 million fewer people are seeing your print ads. If people are throwing away Yellow Pages books, then none of those people are seeing your Yellow Pages directory listing.[9]

Savvy marketers are transferring spending to online advertising—particularly paid search—but they haven't yet started to take full advantage of the 85 percent of clicks that organic search produces.

Buyers Are Shifting to Searching

Our buying patterns are changing along with our online behavior.[10] Of the 18 billion monthly U.S. searches, nearly 12 percent are retail-focused.[11] United States census data from 2008 showed that e-commerce sales reached $31.9 billion that year.[12] Market research company Forrester estimates that the worldwide e-commerce market will reach $235 billion in 2009. Clearly, we've begun buying online. How do we get to those e-commerce sites? In 2007, Microsoft internal research found that 86 percent of searchers start at a major search engine when shopping and 70 percent of those product-related queries are for categories, such as [digital camera].[13]

In part because search has become such a core way in which we navigate the Web, the home page of a site may not be the entry point for a visitor. Any page can be the entry page, which makes it increasingly difficult for marketers to craft messages that welcome visitors and compel them through the conversion funnel. We have to rethink our approach to site design and user interaction based on this new world. (We'll talk more about how to ensure every page of your site is a compelling entry in Chapter 4.)

Even those retailers who don't sell products online or who have substantial offline sales are still impacted by search. Online advertising triggers $6 to be spent offline for every dollar spent online[14] and the in-store sales boost from search is three times greater than online display advertising. Considering that those numbers were calculated for paid search, how much of a greater impact can organic search have with 85 percent of the clicks?

Sixty-three percent of search-related purchases occur offline,[15] and for some categories, this number is even higher.[16] What about local businesses? In a WebVisible/Nielson study, 82 percent of respondents said that they've used the internet to find local businesses; 80 percent say they've researched a product or service online before buying it locally. Yet, only 44 percent of small businesses even have a Web site.[17] If you have a business, you need to be visible in search engines whether you sell online or not.

Paid Search Isn't Enough

As already noted, companies can connect with searchers in two primary ways: *paid search* and *organic search*.

Paid search consists of ads that advertisers can buy to display to searchers who type in particular queries. These ads are labeled "sponsored" on the search results page. These ads can be very targeted (for instance, an advertiser can show an ad that says "buy wool socks here" to a searcher who types in "where can I buy wool socks?") and the order in which the ads appear is based on a number of factors including the amount the advertiser is willing to pay for each click, the relevance of the ad to the query, and the quality of the page linked to in the ad.

Organic search, on the other hand, is comprised of results that are algorithmically generated. Search engines mine the Web, extract the content, assign value and relevance to each page, and then return and

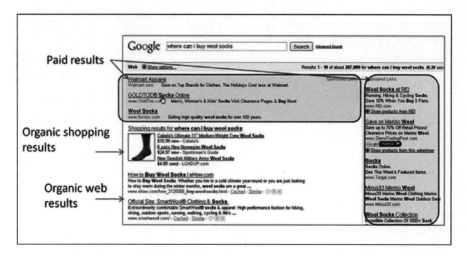

Figure 1.7   Organic Search versus Paid Search

Source: Google Search Results

rank those pages for each query. See Figure 1.7. (You can learn more about this process in Chapter 5.)

Businesses are becoming increasingly savvy about paid search. It's a measurable advertising mechanism by which you can track exactly how much you're spending and what the return is. However, many businesses have not yet invested in organic search because they aren't sure how it works or how to measure it. But whatever the return you are getting from paid search, your organic search return will be greater. And if your site is visible in both paid and organic results, both strategies will provide an even *greater* investment.

Let's take a closer look at the numbers.

Organic Search Performance

Not only do searchers click on organic results 85 percent of the time, an organic listing is between two and six times more visible than a paid one. One hundred percent of searchers look at the first organic result, while only 50 percent look at the first paid result. As the rankings go down, the gap widens: 50 percent of searchers see the seventh organic listing, but only 10 percent of searchers see the seventh paid listing.[18] Even if you're looking for increased brand awareness rather than clicks, organic search will provide a greater return.

In May, 2009, online intelligence-gathering group Hitwise reported that paid search engine traffic to Web sites was down 26 percent from the previous year, yet organic search traffic was up.[19] Research company comScore found that while 2009 U.S. search queries were up 68 percent over the previous year, paid clicks had grown only 18 percent during that same period.[20] In some cases, this was due to a reduction in paid search spending, but this was also the result of changing searcher behavior. Searchers are typing longer queries that trigger fewer paid search matches and they are increasingly recognizing the difference between organic and paid results and have growing ad blindness. Studies have also shown that searchers trust organic listings more than paid ones and that organic results are perceived as most relevant.[21] Additionally, the increasing number of videos and images in search results draws the searcher's attention away from the paid search column.

One considerable advantage of investing in organic search is that it continues to provide value over time, whereas paid search traffic disappears as soon as you stop your spend. Fifty-six percent of Google queries show no paid ads at all, so if you're counting on paid search to provide all of your visibility to searchers, you could be missing half your audience.[22]

The Additional Lift of Ranking in Both Paid and Organic Results

Numerous studies have found that when a site is visible in both paid and organic search results, both results receive more clicks than if either appeared alone. This could be because seeing a brand in both places reinforces the perception that the brand is reputable. It could be because even if we don't consciously process that we've already seen the brand, it seems familiar and, thus, relevant when we see it a second time. Whatever the reason, studies have found that click-through rates, conversion rates, and revenue are all higher when both organic and paid listings appear for a search.[23] An iCrossing study found that when a brand appears in both the organic and paid results, the searcher clicked on that brand 92 percent of the time, compared

TOTAL	CLICKS	increased by 91.80%	PAGE VIEWS	increased by 43.63%
	ACTIONS	increased by 45.00%	VISITORS	increased by 40.69%
	ORDERS	increased by 44.92%	TIME ON SITE	increased by 38.91%

Figure 1.8 iCrossing Study Adding Organic Search Components to a Paid Search Campaign

Source: icrossing.com

to 60 percent of clicks when the brand appeared in only one location.[24] This study found the results show in Figure 1.8 when an organic search component was added to an existing paid search campaign.

A Google-sponsored Enquiro brand study, which focused on consumers in the early stages of purchasing a fuel efficient car who hadn't yet decided on a brand, found that:

- Searchers who saw Honda in the top paid and organic result were 16 percent more likely to think of Honda as a fuel efficient car than when the brand didn't appear in either place.
- Searchers were 42 percent more likely to recall Honda when the brand appeared in both kinds of results versus just the top organic listing.
- Searchers who saw Honda in both organic and paid results were 8 percent more likely to have purchase intent toward Honda and were 26 percent *less* likely to consider a Honda purchase if the brand appeared in neither spot.[25]

You Can Get Ahead of Your Competition by Focusing on Organic Search

The numbers make one thing clear: organic search is a worthwhile investment. But whereas online ad spending continues to grow—at $9.1 billion in 2007, and projected to reach $20.9 billion in 2013[26]—the percentage spent on paid search has outpaced organic between 2004 and 2008 (organic search had 12 percent of marketing spend in 2004 and

10 percent of marketing spend in 2008 at $1.3 billion[27]). Chances are, your competition isn't yet taking full advantage of what organic search can offer and you can take the lead here while they're playing catch up.

Michelle Goldberg, a partner at venture capital firm Ignition Partners, stresses the importance of organic search to the companies she funds:

> *Understanding the differences between paid and organic search and implementing each correctly is critical to the success of an early stage company. Paid search may provide immediate volume, but only provides customers as long as the company pays for clicks. If not done right, a company can spend $1.00 to make $0.95. Organic search is a long term and generally much better margin solution. The largest expense associated with organic search tends to be content creation, which can have long term benefits for both search acquisition and overall customer engagement. Not only is focusing on content creation good for search, but it's also good for users and the business overall because you're creating content that consumers find valuable and that helps you build a more sustainable business over time. I make sure every startup I work with has an organic search strategy.[28]*

How Search Performance Can Impact Offline Ad Campaigns

Advertising (such as TV commercials, radio advertising, print ads, and direct mail) will cause a certain number of potential customers to go into your store, call you, or type your domain name into a browser, but more often than not these days, those potential customers will search for more information. Television commercials in particular can drive search traffic, as over half of us watch TV and surf the internet at the same time.[29] Two-thirds of us are motivated to search due to an offline channel such as a TV ad.[30] Offline advertising can drive searches for both the ad taglines and the products themselves. For instance, Apple started airing "I'm a Mac" ads in 2006, and the search volume for the phrase has steadily gone up ever since (see Figures 1.9 and 1.10).

If Apple had simply aired the commercials expecting consumers to go directly to their stores, they would have missed the entire potential

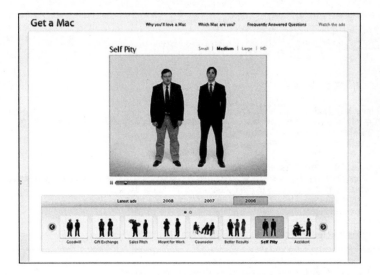

Figure 1.9 Apple's [I'm A Mac] Commercial Reel
Source: Apple.Com

customer base of searchers. But these would-be consumers have a positive experience when they search, as Apple.Com is listed as the first two results for [I'm a Mac] (see Figure 1.11).

However, not all companies enjoy such a successful integration of TV commercials and organic search. During the 2009 Super Bowl, Hyundai spent approximately $13.5 million on advertising by sponsoring

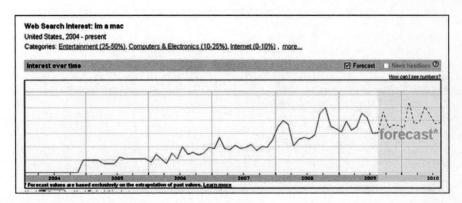

Figure 1.10 [I'm A Mac] Search Volume
Source: Google Insights For Search

Google i'm a mac   (Search) Advanced Search

Web ⊞ Show options...

Apple - Get a Mac - Watch the TV Ads
Watch all the latest TV ads for **Mac**. ... Test-drive new products with a **Mac** Specialist at the
Apple Retail Store. Personal Shopping ...
www.apple.com/getamac/ads/ - Cached - Similar - 💬 ⊼ ⊠

  Apple - Get a Mac
  Check out the top reasons why you'll love a **Mac**. Find out which **Mac** is right for you. See
  how easy it is to move to **Mac**. And watch the latest TV ads.
  Watch the ads - Which Mac are you - How to move to Mac - Store
  www.apple.com/getamac/ - Cached - Similar - 💬 ⊼ ⊠

  ⊞ Show more results from www.apple.com

Figure 1.11   Google Search Results: [I'm A Mac]
Source: Google Search Results

the pregame show and running ads throughout the game. Two of its
commercials centered on its new coupe (at $6 million for airing costs,
plus commercial production costs). It first appeared that Hyundai under-
stood how to integrate offline and online activities and recognized their
customers' desire to interact with the company online. The ad showed
the car speeding around a racetrack with exciting imagery and video and
ended with a Web site: edityourown.com. See Figure 1.12.

Figure 1.12   Hyundai "Edit Your Own" Commercial
Source: Personal Screencap

The site combined interactive elements and social media components and enabled visitors to create their own videos that starred the Hyundai Genesis Coupe and share them with their friends. Clearly, the ad was intended to drive visitors to the "Edit Your Own" site and it's likely that the marketing team responsible for the campaign measured the commercial's success in part based on site traffic.

How well did the ad do? It probably did cause some viewers to type edityourown.com into their browser's address bar, but it also did something else. It caused viewers to search. Not long after the commercial aired, Google's Hot Trends showed that interest spiked for both [Hyundai genesis coupe] and [edit your own]. See Figures 1.13 and 1.14.

Did searchers find what they were looking for when they typed [edit your own] into Google? Not exactly.

Someone looking for edityourown.com would have likely been disappointed, since that domain doesn't appear anywhere in Google search results. To Hyundai's credit, it did buy a search ad for the query, so even though it doesn't appear in the organic results, it does appear on the page. Unfortunately, since the ad shows the hyundaigenesis.com domain rather than edityourown.com, many searchers might have overlooked it and assumed it wasn't what they were looking for. And since we're an

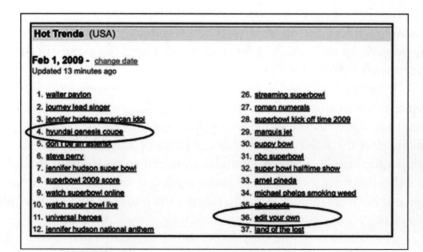

Figure 1.13   Google Search Trends, Super Bowl 2009
Source: Google Trends

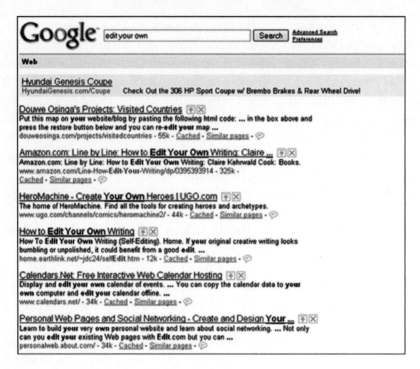

Figure 1.14   Google Search Results: [Edit Your Own]

Source: Google Search Results

instant-gratification culture as well as a searching culture, many people likely gave up and simply went back to watching the game after their failed attempt to find the site.

It's clear from the Google Trends data that the commercial spiked interest in the campaign, but if the marketing department measured success only based on site visits, it may have considered the commercial a failure. But the failure occurred at the point of search—not due to the commercial itself. Though Hyundai appeared to understand the relationship between offline and online media, it was missing a crucial piece—that of organic search. Harnessing the power of that relationship is a primary strategy you'll learn in this book.

Hyundai wasn't the only Super Bowl advertiser that could have benefited from a better search acquisition strategy. Consider this snapshot of Google Trends during the last few minutes of the game. Google Trends tracks searches that have substantial spikes in query volume over

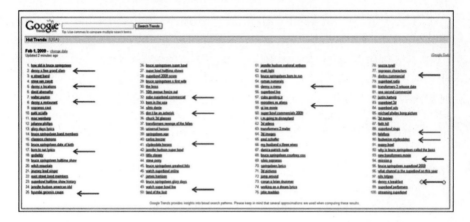

Figure 1.15   Google Search Trends, Super Bowl 2009 Commercial Search Spikes
Source: Google Trends

a short period of time. In the last moments of the Super Bowl, 16 of the top 100 spiking searches were related to Super Bowl commercials.[31] See Figure 1.15.

When I did those searches myself to build a Super Bowl commercial scorecard, I found that many had results that may as well have been a locked door and a closed sign.

Reverse Advertising: Avoiding the Advertising Death Spiral

Marketers have been bemoaning the rising problems with traditional advertising for years. Marty Neumeier, author of *Zag: The Number One Strategy of High-Performance Brands* and *The Brand Gap*, describes the "advertising death spiral"[32] during which consumers filter out advertising because it's not relevant to their current task. In turn, advertisers get louder, causing consumers to filter more and advertisers to yell even louder. (This filter occurs online,[33] as well as offline.)

Marketer Seth Godin, in his book, *Permission Marketing*, calls the traditional advertising methods of blasting a scattershot message to a large group of people (through such channels as radio and TV ads) who may or may not be interested in your product "interruption advertising."[34] But what's the alternative?

The answer: let your potential customers tell *you* what they are looking for. This way, you won't interrupt your potential audience from the task they're focusing on in order to get their attention. Instead, what you have to offer *is* crucial to their current task. Search provides results that are relevant to the activity in progress and searchers are filtering out everything else to concentrate on that. You won't have to fight for the viewer's attention and convince them they need a product (and all the while risk the advertising death spiral). Instead, you can focus on convincing this purchase-ready group that they should buy *your* product.

Danny Sullivan, one of the first search engine industry experts, calls the process of acquisition from search "reverse advertising."[35] You simply find out what the members of your target audience are looking for, and then meet their needs and wait for them to come to you. Someone typing [fuel efficient cars] into a Google search box is much more likely to be considering purchasing a car than someone who's sitting on the couch watching *The Oprah Winfrey Show*.

Reverse Advertising in Action   To see reverse advertising in action, consider an auto manufacturer. We'll use Volvo as our example and assume that Volvo is targeting its V70 wagon to moms who don't want to drive a minivan and who are looking for safety, as well as room for two children. Volvo might opt to buy expensive TV ads that showcase these features during time slots that its target demographic is watching (such as during *Oprah*). However, only a percentage of that audience meets the target demographic (men and single women watch the show as well). And within the target demographic, only a small percentage is interested in buying a car.

Buying television ads might be a worthwhile investment, both to drive sales and raise brand awareness, but consider the additional acquisition opportunities available through the reverse advertising of organic search.

Using search data, Volvo compiles a list of what its target audience is interested in during the quest for a new car and what the audience searches for. The company adds this content to its Web site and uses the information in this book to ensure that that content appears for those searches. In this way, it connects with exactly the customers who are looking for the company at the exact moment those customers are focused on its product. And it ensures brand awareness by having visibility in that critical moment in the buying cycle when its competitor could have dominated.

Rather than just talking at a large group of people, hoping some of them will listen, this approach enables Volvo to be the listener and provide information to the right people at the right time.

How Search Has Changed Business

Historically, consumer data and industry trends haven't been that easy to come by. Before launching a new product or feature, companies had to rely on expensive and time-consuming surveys and focus groups, and it often took awhile to gather enough feedback from these sources. Competitive and industry research was slow and expensive. But the abundance of search data has allowed all of that to change dramatically. We can see *exactly* what our customers want at a much larger scale than focus groups could ever provide, and competitive and industry data is just a click or two away. We can get immediate feedback about whether changes are working and see trends of consumer interest rising or falling before we invest in R&D. (We'll dive into the details of how search data can provide insight about our customers, our industry, and our competitors in Chapter 2.)

Search Data as Market Research

Continuing our earlier Volvo example, search data indicates that the audience most likely to buy a Volvo V70 is searching most for "reliable" and "safe." See Figure 1.16.

Keywords	Advertiser Competition ⑦	▼ Local Search Volume: July ⑦	Global Monthly Search Volume ⑦
Keywords related to term(s) entered - sort by relevance ⑦			
reliable cars	▬▬▬◻	33,100	22,200
reliable car	▬▬◻	22,200	18,100
most reliable cars	▬▬◻	18,100	12,100
safe cars	▬▬▬◻	14,800	12,100

Figure 1.16   [Reliable] and [Safe] Search Volume
Source: Google Adwords

Keywords	Advertiser Competition ⑦	▼ Local Search Volume: July ⑦	Global Monthly Search Volume ⑦
Keywords related to term(s) entered - sort by relevance ⑦			
family car	▭	135,000	110,000
car for kids	▭	60,500	49,500
cars for kids	▭	49,500	40,500

Figure 1.17 [Family Car] Search Volume

Source: Google Adwords

This audience also tends to search for [family car]. See Figure 1.17.

Based on this data, our hypothetical Volvo marketing department creates two pages of content in the V70 section of its Web site. One is about the V70's safety and reliability and includes crash test ratings, safety scores, and comparisons to other cars that this demographic may be considering. The other is all about how great the V70 is for kids. It provides back seat dimensions and shows photos of different passenger configurations involving car seats and adult passengers. Then, rather than (or in addition to) broadcasting this content out to everyone, Volvo waits for its key demographic to find it.

Someone typing [most reliable family car] into a search box is much more likely to intend to buy a car in the near future—and a kid-friendly one, at that—than someone watching a television show with the "right demographics." Volvo connects with a potential consumer who is broadcasting his or her purchasing intent and actively looking for a car just like the Volvo V70. Not only does Volvo connect with the right audience, it can actively compete in an acquisition channel that may have otherwise only included its competition.

Focusing on search doesn't mean that you should abandon your other acquisition efforts. In fact, organic search can work hand-in-hand with other marketing efforts. That commercial during *Oprah* may increase brand awareness, which in turn makes the searcher more likely to click on that Volvo result later, rather than the Toyota listing.

If You're Not Among Consumers' Choices, They Can't Choose You

Consider the case of UK airline BMI, whose primary customers live in the UK and Ireland. A substantial number (including me) live in other countries and are planning trips to the UK. I was in Seattle, planning a trip to Ireland and looking for a flight from London to Dublin. Since I had flown this BMI route before, it was the most prominent brand in my mind as I started my search. I searched for [Heathrow to Dublin] and didn't see the BMI site. However, Aer Lingus appeared third in the results of my search (see Figure 1.18).

Even though BMI was the brand that I recalled most vividly when I began my search, it wasn't available for consideration when I made my choice, and Aer Lingus was an easy alternative.

But what if I pressed on, determined to include BMI in my consideration set? A search for its brand name, [BMI], doesn't return its site in the results either (although a fairly negative news article about them *does* appear). If potential customers can't even find you in a brand search, you are missing one of the most qualified channels of customer acquisition.

We've seen how search data can provide a wealth of market research and enable you to connect with customers early in their research cycle—at the very time that they're looking to buy your product. In the following chapters, we'll learn how to put that information in action.

Figure 1.18   Google Search Results: [Heathrow to Dublin Flight]
Source: Google Search Results

The Level Playing Field of Search

If you're under the impression that only big brands can compete in the game of search, you'll be pleasantly surprised to learn that smaller companies can often have the advantage. This is particularly true when potential customers are conducting non-branded searches—that is, searches for [safe cars] rather than [Volvo]—because they evaluate choices based on the results they see. Large companies aren't always nimble enough to take full advantage of what search has to offer and a smaller company can often beat a larger one in the rankings. Unlike TV advertising and other large-scale marketing campaigns, companies don't require a huge budget to compete in organic search. They simply need the knowledge to build an effective search strategy. In fact, a comScore study found that market segments with smaller consumer bases (for which a scattershot approach such as TV advertising wouldn't be cost effective) can use search for significant lift to a very targeted population.[36]

For smaller organizations, organic search can provide a low-cost way to build a highly targeted audience. Avvo, a Seattle startup that provides an online legal directory for consumers, found that even though they were a small company, they were able to quickly build a large audience through organic search by adding search engine optimization (SEO) best practices throughout their organization. Conrad Saam, Vice President of Marketing for Avvo notes that not only was integrating an organic search strategy into their business effective, but it complemented and enhanced their focus on quality content and an engaging user experience.

"We launched Avvo in 2007 to fill a content gap on the web— helping consumers make informed, intelligent decisions about their legal situation. In doing that, we adhered to the most fundamental SEO principle—build a great product and fill it with content that people care about. Our primary focus was on providing consumers with something they really needed. SEO was baked into everything we did to ensure that all great content got to the people who were looking for it. We think about the search impact of everything we do—from marketing to product development, to public relations, and

even customer service. In two years, we became the most popular legal directory on the web—more popular than our huge corporate competitors with massive advertising budgets. In the end, it was much more effective to develop a robust, useful, and searchable site than to buy TV spots on CNN."[37]

Large brands can also use this knowledge to their advantage, if they can evolve their businesses to integrate search and changing customer behaviors into their product and customer acquisition strategies.

But whether you run a multinational corporation or a Napa Valley bed and breakfast, where do you start? You might be anxious about making the right move if you don't have a background in online marketing or data analysis. Well, you can relax. This book will give you everything you need to get started creating a business strategy that takes full advantage of everything that search has to offer and builds this knowledge into your organization.

CHAPTER

How to Use Search Data to Improve Your Business and Product Strategy

Searchers aren't an isolated demographic from the rest of your target audience. Searchers *are* your target audience. And they're telling you exactly what will compel them to buy your products, engage with your company, and become your strongest advocates.

The largest source of this data is through the major search engines, particularly Google. Millions of people search using these search engines every day, and in aggregate what they search for and how those searches change over time provides incredibly useful insight into their needs.

Just as valuable as the words they type are the ways they behave. Search engines know exactly what people click on after they enter a query. They know what content searchers viewed then quickly returned to the search results to look for a better answer. They can follow the entire search session to better understand intent: What did the searcher type next? What result did the searcher click on that ended the search?[1]

Research companies like Enquiro Research augment this understanding of searcher intent with data about what searchers see as they scan the search results and what they focus on, as well as what they skip. And research into how the brain processes information as we search helps complete the picture of what searchers are really after.

Marrying *how* we search (behavior) with *why* we search (intent) and *what* we search for (query volume) is vital to understanding a business's potential audience, since the average length of a query is three words, and many queries consist of only one word.[2] It's difficult to know intent for many one-word queries. But coupled with search history, aggregate behaviors, and other behavioral data, the intent picture becomes much clearer.

If you can track individual behavior and add this information to the rest of the data, you can get a very clear picture indeed. (You can learn more about tracking visitors on your site in Chapter 8.)

How We Use Search for Research: Planning a Trip to Lake Tahoe

A Microsoft search session in February, 2009, that lasted nearly four hours and included eight queries and 27 visited sites illustrates how searcher intent is difficult to discern from a single query and how results found in earlier queries can influence later ones. See Figure 2.1.

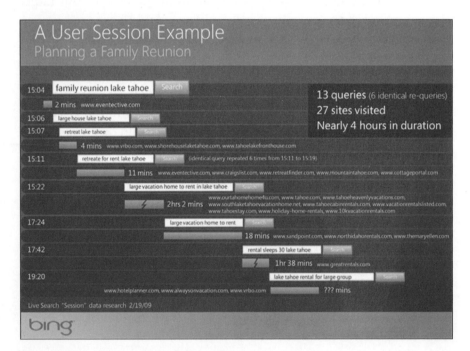

Figure 2.1   Microsoft Bing Search Session
Source: Microsoft Bing

The searcher begins the search with [family reunion Lake Tahoe]. The results generally relate to event planning, which is clearly not what the searcher is looking for, as subsequent searches are more obviously related to lodging ([large house Lake Tahoe], [large vacation home to rent in Lake Tahoe]). The searcher originally was focused on the outcome of his task—having a family reunion in Lake Tahoe—but he quickly realized that the way to reach that goal was to look for lodging that would accommodate many people (the last query in the session is [Lake Tahoe rental for large group]). At one point, he searches for [rental sleeps 30 Lake Tahoe]. If you were tracking individual visitor behavior, then when this visitor landed on your site for [Lake Tahoe rental for large group], you'd know that he's bringing 30 people for a family reunion and he'd like a large house to accommodate everyone.

This type of data may not be all that valuable for your business based on one visitor. But what if you found that you had highest conversion rates from [Lake Tahoe large rental], that 80 percent of those conversions were from searchers who had previously searched for family reunion–related content, and that most searchers doing that same [Lake Tahoe large rental] search who had previously searched for [college spring break] didn't convert at all?

Depending on other data, you might build out a family reunion resources section to attract even more of the high converting customers and you might create a page describing why the rental is great for college students on spring break (if that's an audience you'd like to convert).

Of course testing is key to make sure it works.

Market Research: Where the Wild Frontiers of Human Nature Meet the Wild Powers of Technology

In his book *Spent*, biological psychologist Geoffrey Miller talks about his experience at a 1999 conference about economic preferences. The economists in attendance were more interested in buying patterns than the psychological reasons behind them. However, the marketers in attendance *did* care, leading Miller down a road of research about marketing at the end of which he concluded: "Marketing is not just one of the most important ideas in business. It has become the most dominant force in human culture." He defines marketing as "[a] systematic attempt to fulfill human desires by producing goods and services that people will buy. It is where the wild frontiers of human nature meet the wild powers of technology." And he describes the marketing revolution of the 1950s and 60s as a shift to understanding that a "company should produce what people desire, instead of trying to convince them to buy what the company happens to make."[3]

The discipline of market research was born and is now an $8 billion industry in the United States alone.[4]

Before the Web, it was difficult to learn about what large groups of people were interested in without conducting large scale surveys. But today, nearly all of your potential customers are broadcasting exactly what they want through their searches. And search data may even be more honest than survey data, since people are searching for what they actually want, not telling a surveyor what they think they should want.

Miller notes that not all industries have embraced this method of creating products (such as banking, law, and medicine) and concludes that those who don't "bother using market research to shape their services to their customers' desires, [will] lose market share to those that do."

The same can be said of search data. Those businesses that don't realize that we've experienced a shift in consumer behavior and that customers and customer data are now centered on search will lose market share to those that do.

Miller says that "marketing knowledge lurks as a sort of arcane magic," and the same can definitely be said of search-based consumer acquisition.

With search data, we can gain new insights into our customers, our industry, and our competitors, but many businesses think of it as a kind of arcane magic that they aren't sure how to best harness. But once you know where to get the data and how to apply it, you'll find that search data provides clear insight that makes running your business and acquiring customers easier, smoother, and more measurable.

Search Acquisition Strategy: The New Product Strategy and Customer Acquisition Strategy

Effective search acquisition begins with learning more about your customers and what they're searching for. From there, you can assess your site and make sure it satisfies the needs of those searchers. Finally, you ensure that when your customers search, your site shows up in results. It stands to reason then that search acquisition strategy is really customer acquisition strategy and, at its core, product strategy.

The biggest difference between traditional market research and search-based market research is that you can gain a great deal of information about customer behavior and needs without spending a dime on focus groups, surveys, or other expensive methods. That doesn't mean you won't do some of those things to refine your strategy and confirm your conclusions or as a parallel endeavor, but an amazing amount of data is available from search and, with multivariate testing and mouse movement tracking, you can see how customers are responding in near-real time.[5]

Building a Better Digital Camera

Consider a new digital camera manufacturer, BetterCamera. They are looking to build the right set of features into their inaugural product. But what do people care about most in a camera? The product development team at BetterCamera can gain some insight into what that might be by looking at search logs.

First, how big is the digital camera market? According to Google, over 41 million people searched for [camera digital] and [digital cameras] in July 2009.[6] And that number doesn't include all of the variations of related searches such as specific digital camera brand names.

According to Google AdWords, the top searched-for digital camera features are:

- SLR
- Waterproof
- Lenses
- Underwater
- Size
- Pixels

BetterCamera hasn't had breakthroughs with its lens technology that would rival the competition, and its megapixel and size specs are comparable to other brands. The company decides to explore the idea of building an underwater (and thus waterproof) camera.

The BetterCamera team uses search data for a bit of competitive research and finds that the top searched-for brands for waterproof and digital cameras are:

- Olympus
- Canon
- Fuji
- Nikon

This is an area that the team feels it can compete in because only a small number of searchers are looking for specific brands. Most are looking for simply variations of [waterproof digital cameras] and [underwater digital cameras]. See Figure 2.2.

Could BetterCamera gain insight into the audience for waterproof and underwater cameras and what features are most important to them? The first thing the product team notices is that, not surprisingly, search interest spikes in summer. And overall interest isn't declining, which confirms the underwater digital camera business is a healthy one. See Figure 2.3.

Searchers in Hawaii and Florida appear most interested in underwater cameras, but third-place Alaska is unexpected. The market research

Keywords	Advertiser Competition ⑦	Local Search Volume: August ⑦
Keywords related to term(s) entered - sort by relevance ⑦		
waterproof digital camera		550,000
underwater digital camera		135,000
canon waterproof digital camera		90,500
waterproof digital cameras		60,500
olympus waterproof digital camera		74,000
underwater digital cameras		33,100
underwater digital camera housing		18,100
canon underwater digital camera		9,900
canon underwater digital cameras		9,900
nikon underwater digital camera		3,600
olympus underwater digital camera		4,400

Figure 2.2   [Underwater Camera] Search Volume
Source: Google Adwords

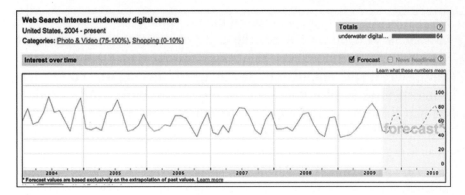

Figure 2.3   [Underwater Digital Camera] Search Trends
Source: Google Insights for Search

team will have to look more closely into that. Are these searches driven primarily by Alaskans planning vacations to tropical destinations? See Figure 2.4.

Looking at specific searches, the BetterCamera team finds that those in the market for an underwater digital camera are particularly interested in disposable versions, waterproof housings, and inexpensive options. Perhaps the company should consider offering low-cost

Regional interest		
1. Hawaii	━━━━━━━━	100
2. Florida	━━	32
3. Alaska	━━	27
4. California	━	20
5. Colorado	━	19
6. New Jersey	━	18
7. Washington	━	18
8. Oregon	━	17
9. Texas	━	17
10. Arizona	━	16

Figure 2.4   [Underwater Digital Cameras] Regional Search Trends
Source: Google Insights for Search

alternatives to expensive waterproof digital cameras for those potential customers who only need to take pictures underwater during short vacations and, therefore, aren't looking to invest in high-cost solutions. But quality is still important to this audience (after all, why take underwater pictures at all if they aren't going to turn out?), so the product team at Better Camera looks into designing a waterproof housing that will enable the two-week-a-year scuba divers to turn their existing high-quality digital cameras into underwater versions.

Some of this potential audience clearly knows that buying a waterproof housing is an option based on the high volume of existing searches, so a consumer base already exists. In addition, the BetterCamera team brainstorms ways of marketing to the audience segment looking for inexpensive and disposable underwater digital cameras. After all, the number of monthly Google searches for waterproof housings is approximately 40,000, whereas the number of Google searches for waterproof digital cameras is around 600,000. So if the team only went after those already looking for waterproof housings, it would be neglecting a substantial target market. See Figure 2.5.

Keywords	Advertiser Competition ⑦	Local Search Volume: August ⑦
Keywords related to term(s) entered - <u>sort by relevance</u> ⑦		
waterproof digital camera		550,000
underwater digital camera		135,000
canon waterproof digital camera		90,500
waterproof digital cameras		60,500
olympus waterproof digital camera		74,000
underwater digital cameras		33,100
underwater digital camera housing		18,100
canon underwater digital camera		9,900
underwater housing for digital camera		6,600
waterproof digital camera housing		12,100
nikon underwater digital camera		3,600
olympus underwater digital camera		4,400

Figure 2.5 [Underwater Digital Camera] Search Trends

Source: Google Insights for Search

Search Data: A Powerful Source of Market Research

With all the searching your potential customers are doing, you can gain a great deal of information about exactly what they're looking for.

And we get more than just a list of queries from search data. We can find out what searchers looked for next, where they were searching from, and what they were searching for most.

Using Keyword Research for Market Insights

As you saw with BetterCamera, you can use keyword research to determine the keywords with the highest query volumes, which have the most competition and which are most likely to attract searchers to your site and turn them into customers.

How Keyword Research Is Valuable

- You gain insight into what searches have the highest volume (and can bring the most traffic).
- You get data on the competitive landscape of each query category.
- You learn the language of the customer, so you can better engage them (in clicking on the search result, staying on the page, and converting).
- You can better prioritize features and content additions based on expected traffic lifts.

Predicting Future Trends

But how reliable is search data in predicting future trends and influencing business decisions? The Google research team has spent a great deal of time considering this. As the team noted in its blog:

> *Having predictable trends for a search query or for a group of queries could have interesting ramifications. One could forecast the trends*

into the future, and use it as a "best guess" for various business decisions such as budget planning, marketing campaigns and resource allocations. One could identify deviation from such forecasting and identify new factors that are influencing the search volume. We were therefore interested in the following questions:

- *How many search queries have trends that are predictable?*
- *Are some categories more predictable than others? How is the distribution of predictable trends between the various categories?*
- *How predictable are the trends of aggregated search queries for different categories? Which categories are more predictable and which are less so?*[7]

From this investigation, the team published a paper that describes how its research found that, among other things:[8]

- Over half of the most popular Google search queries are predictable in a 12-month forecast. Categories such as health, food and drink, and travel have the highest percentage of predictable queries.
- The rest are not predictable (which makes sense, as Google can't predict who will be the next Britney Spears or Twitter). Entertainment, for instance, has a low percentage of predictable queries.
- Eighty-eight percent of the aggregated category search trends of over 600 categories in Insights for Search, one of Google's free keyword research tools, are predictable.[9]

Based on this research, Google launched the forecasting feature for Google Insights, which predicts future search volume for those queries in which it has some degree of confidence. (You'll see this feature in action later in this chapter.)

In its paper *Predicting the Present With Google Trends*, the team found that "Google Trends data *can* help improve forecasts of the current level of activity for a number of different economic time series, including automobile sales, home sales, and travel behavior."[10]

Look, for instance at the search trends for Figure 2.6.

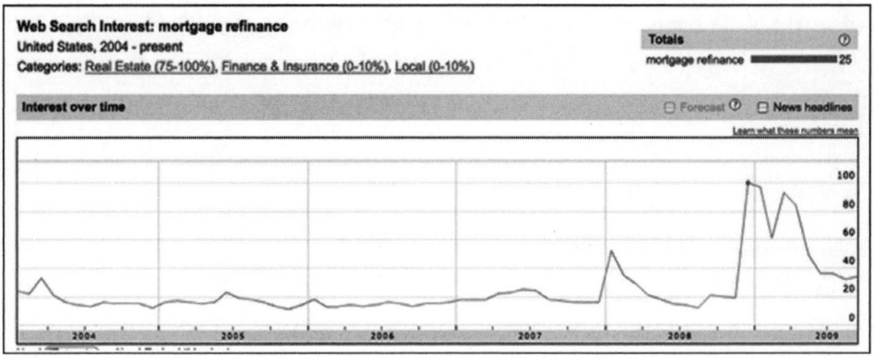

Figure 2.6 [Mortgage Refinance] Search Trends

Source: Google Insights for Search

Interest spiked sharply in late 2008 and began to decline in the latter half of 2009.

This data can also provide competitive research, diving into the top searches shows that [Wells Fargo] is the dominant searched-for bank (see Figure 2.7). And the data can provide product strategy insights as well. If we want to attract searchers to our mortgage products, we'd be wise to provide a mortgage calculator.

Google says it expects this forecasting data to help businesses make decisions about budget planning, marketing campaigns, and resource

Search terms

Top searches		Rising searches	
1. refinance rates	100	1. refinance my mortgage	+140%
2. refinance mortgage rates	100	2. should i refinance	+130%
3. mortgage rates	100	3. wells fargo mortgage	+120%
4. refinance home	45	4. wells fargo refinance	+100%
5. home mortgage refinance	45	5. refinance mortgage rates	+90%
6. home mortgage	45	6. refinance rates	+80%
7. refinance calculator	35	7. mortgage rates	+80%
8. mortgage refinance calculator	35	8. how to refinance	+80%
9. mortgage calculator	35	9. mortgage rates current	+70%
10. refinance loan	30	10. refinance fha mortgage	+60%

Figure 2.7 [Mortgage Refinance] Top Search Terms

Source: Google Insights for Search

allocations. If tools powered by such high volumes of customer data exist for free to help you gain insight into your market planning, marketing campaigns, and resource allocations, don't you want to take advantage of them?

Search Data as Economic Indicator

A September, 2009 Washington Post story described Google chief economist Hal Varian's efforts to lobby government agencies to use Google search tools to better understand "customer sentiment, corporate health, and social interests." Varian said he was confident of the national economic recovery—not because of government data, but because of search data. He noted that in March, 2009, the number of Google searches about unemployment benefits and centers began to drop (corresponding to the decline of new jobless claims): "As a contemporaneous predictor, predicting the present through search queries has been a pretty good predictor of initial (jobless) claims."[11]

He also noted an increase in home and real estate agent searches, which he felt indicated a strengthening housing market. He compared this to rising interest earlier in the year for the government's "cash for clunkers" program that he said the government could have used to forecast budgetary needs for the program. (The government underestimated demand and initially didn't allocate the budget necessary to keep up.)

Government agencies might be slow to embrace innovation, but you can be nimble and adopt Varian's advice as it applies to your business. Search data can provide a powerful point of triangulation for other corporate data, market research, and industry trends, and can predict potential industry changes early. By paying attention to how your customers are searching, you can get a jump on the competition, who might not realize such data exists.

Seasonality and Prediction

Google research has found that many queries are seasonal, and can therefore be fairly reliably predicted. (Those who searched for skiing conditions last winter are likely to search for them this winter as well.)

You can see how the forecasting works with the query in Figure 2.8.

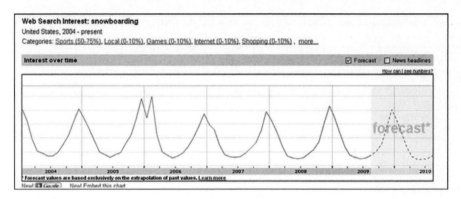

Figure 2.8 [Snowboarding] Search Trends
Source: Google Insights for Search

    If you have a seasonal business, search data can help you pinpoint just when demand is likely to peak. Even if you don't think your business is impacted by seasonality, this trend data can help you be sure.

Using Search Data for Better Business Strategy and Stronger Customer Engagement

The following example formulates a business strategy for a hypothetical bed and breakfast in Sonoma County, CA. (We take a closer look at some of the tools available for conducting this research on page 43, and you can find a comprehensive list of resources at marketingintheageof google.com.)

Business Goals

Before you dive into search data, you should clearly define your business goals. For the B&B, we'll answer the questions as follows:

- What is the primary goal of the business?
  - → To book guests into the B&B.
- What does success look like?
  - → 70 percent occupancy at 90 percent of list prices.

- What is the primary goal of the Web site?
  - → To attract potential guests to book rooms.
- What are the secondary goals of the Web site?
  - → To engage with guests so they have a positive experience and return.
  - → To reduce manual overhead of providing maps, directions, nearby wineries, restaurants, etc. by having all of the information available on the Web site.
- Who is the primary audience of the business?
  - → Those interested in B&Bs who want to tour wineries in Sonoma and who can afford to pay list prices.

The answers to these questions provide us with a foundation: Who is interested in winery tours in Sonoma and like to stay in B&Bs? Where do they live? What do they like? What are they looking for in a B&B?

Knowing this information can help us make the Web site compelling for the audiences so they'll book a room, as well as help us craft the B&B itself so that it meets the needs of the guests. Web strategy and business strategy intertwine. The customers are the same. Their needs are the same. What compels them is the same. What you as a business owner want them to do is the same.

General Trends

How is the B&B business in wine country doing these days? For that, we can check Google Trends (see Figure 2.9).

The first thing we see is that the interest in B&Bs is down slightly, but we also find that many more people are searching for [bed and breakfast] than [b&b].

We also find that people are searching for both Sonoma and Napa and that, whereas searches for Sonoma spike at the end of each year, Napa searches stay fairly constant (see Figure 2.10).

The searches for [wine country] have similar spikes (see Figure 2.11).

We'll have to keep those spikes in mind when we start planning promotions. (Digging further, it seems that the spikes are due to searchers looking to buy Christmas gifts.)

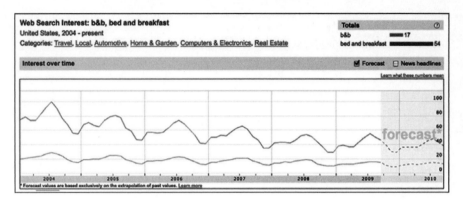

Figure 2.9 [B&B] and [Bed and Breakfast] Search Trends

Source: Google Insights for Search

Where should we target those promotions? We can see that, not surprisingly, Californians have the most interest, followed by those in other nearby states. But both Minnesota and Maine show higher than expected interest for their distances.

Interest is highest in the United States, but there's substantial interest from Canada, as well as other countries (see Figure 2.12).

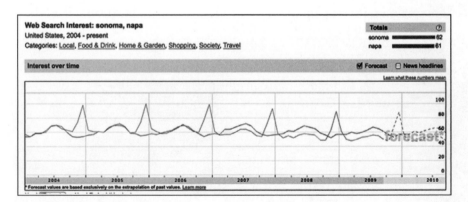

Figure 2.10 [Sonoma] and [Napa] Search Trends

Source: Google Insights for Search

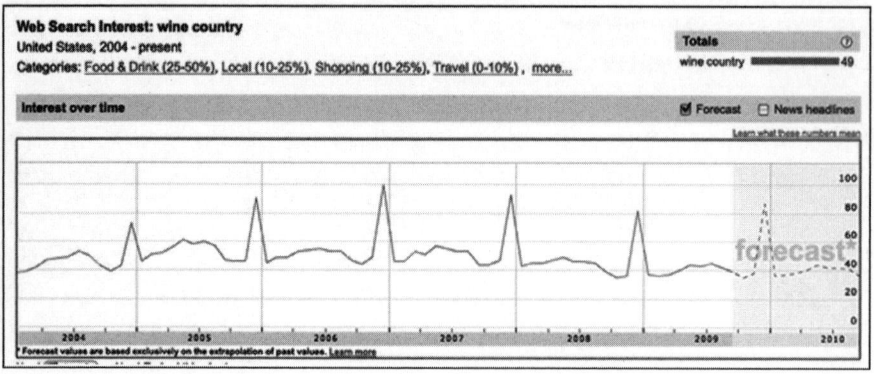

Figure 2.11 [Wine Country] Regional Search Trends
Source: Google Insights for Search

Diving into the top search terms and rising searches, we see that people seem to be interested in:

- Wine country maps
- Visitor information
- Airport information
- Weather
- Wine
- Hotels
- Wine country packages, vacations, and gift baskets

This gives us a starting point for considering how to position our B&B.

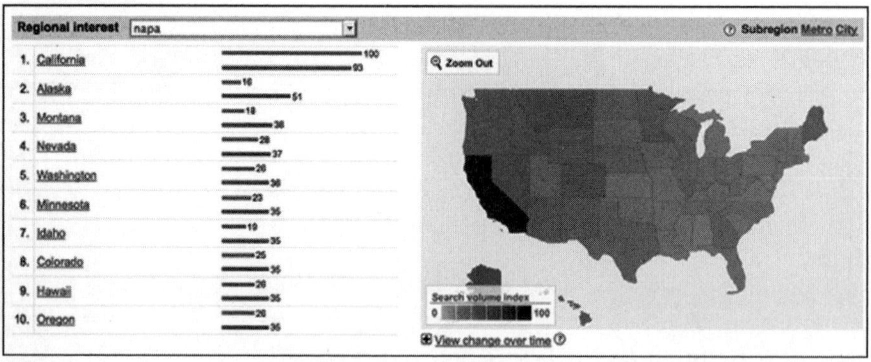

Figure 2.12 [Napa] Regional Search Trends
Source: Google Insights for Search

We know we want to include visitor information on our site (such as maps, airport details, and weather), but we may also want to consider providing vacation packages and even creating gift baskets that can be ordered online. Since gift baskets aren't our core competency, however, we'll hold that idea for when we're ready to expand.

Diving Into Keyword Research

Before we get started, a few words about numbers. Although most keyword tools list numbers, you shouldn't think of them as exact counts. Rather, you should think of them as a way to compare terms on a relative scale. Google clusters and approximates its numbers and many of the other tools use sampling. So, for instance, if Google lists [Napa Valley] at 823,000 queries, [Napa hotels] at 246,000 queries, and [wine country inn] at 14,800 queries, you can conclude that more searches were done for [Napa Valley] and [wine country inn] had substantially fewer queries. But you can't conclude that Google saw exactly 14,800 searches for [wine country inn].

Another thing to keep in mind is that you'll see a lot of references to "keywords" but what this really means is "queries." A "keyword" might actually consist of several words.

Many free and fee-based keyword research tools exist. The search engine tools are generally based on paid search data and are often presented as relative rather than as absolute. Third-party tools tend to be based on data from internet service providers, toolbars, or consumer panels.

We now have an initial seed list of words for our B&B based on our business goals, target audience, and trends information. Based on this seed list, we can build an expanded list with volume information.

Determining Keywords to Use

We've already gotten started with this for our B&B. But there are lots of ways to develop seed lists, including:

- Industry trends
- Existing targets

- Analytics data (which we'll discuss more in Chapter 8)
- Site search logs
- Webmaster Tools data
- Competitor primary keywords (we'll talk about competitive research on page 49)
- Related sites, social media sites in related topics, and other written publications to find out what the audience is interested in
- Data from all of the departments in your organization that deal with customer needs (including product research, customer support, marketing, and PR)—what data can be shared?

We'll start with the Google AdWords Keyword Tool[12] (which you don't need an AdWords account to use). Enter your initial seed list of words and keep "enable synonyms" checked to get an expanded list. You'll get back a list of queries with search volumes based on "broad match." Broad match means that the listed word(s) appeared somewhere in the query. You can switch this list to "exact match," which lists only exact queries.

For instance, we see that the local search volume for [Napa Valley] in August 2009, was 823,000. But this doesn't mean that 823,000 searches were for [Napa Valley]. It simply means that many queries included the words "Napa" and "Valley" ([Napa Valley lodging] and [Napa Valley wineries] would both be counted in this number).

In addition to showing local (which is based on the chosen country and language, which you can change) and global search volumes, this tool also generates advertiser competition information.

Google generates two lists of keywords: related keywords and additional keywords to consider. An easy way to work with these lists is to export them to Excel, sort them by volume, filter out the queries that don't align with your business goals and target audience, and then categorize them. Once you have a general sense of what you're looking for, you can take a look at exact matches.

We can do this with our bed and breakfast data.

As we categorize the queries, patterns start to emerge. Not surprisingly, these searchers are interested in regional activities such as wine tours, trains, restaurants, and spas. They are looking for B&Bs that are historic, luxurious, and romantic. We may decide to partner with a local spa and offer lodging and spa packages. And we may want to decorate at least one of our rooms in romantic tones and offer a romance package, complete with wine train tour.

We also can see smaller details about how people search. They are much more likely to use the abbreviation "CA" than to spell out "California." And they're much more likely to search for "bed and breakfast" than for "bed & breakfast" or "B&B." These may seem like small points, but when you consider that major search engines are still, at their core, text based—matching up queries to pages—you realize that how you word content can make a big difference. Using the language of your customer can help you engage with them better as well.

Use of language becomes even more important with companies selling products that may inadvertently lapse into corporate speak and alienate their potential customers. (We'll talk more about using the language of your customers in Chapter 4.)

Now we have a general sense of how we should position our B&B and how we should talk about it. What else can the data tell us?

We can get a list of questions that people are asking from the WordTracker Keyword Questions Tool.[13] From this, we see that the most asked questions about Napa Valley include:

- Where to go in Napa Valley
- Where to stay in Napa Valley
- What vineyards do you recommend Napa Valley
- When do they harvest grapes in Napa Valley
- Where is the Napa Valley
- What vineyards should you go to in Napa Valley
- Where is the Napa Valley in California
- Where is Napa Valley
- Where is Napa Valley vs San Francisco
- Where is a visitor guide for Napa Valley
- What to do in California Napa Valley
- What is the best winery in Napa Valley
- When is harvest time in the wine country Napa Valley
- What to wear in Napa Valley
- When is the best time to visit Napa Valley
- What airport do you fly into for the Napa Valley

- Where to taste Napa Valley cult wines
- What is closest city to Napa Valley
- How far is Napa Valley from San Diego
- When to go to Napa Valley
- What to do in the Napa Valley

We can learn at least a couple of things from this list. We see that people are looking for:

- Where to stay in Napa Valley
- Location and direction information about Napa Valley
- The best time to visit Napa Valley
- Things to do in Napa Valley

We also see how people craft their queries. We may want to include copy on our site such as "looking for where to stay in Napa Valley?" Be sure to use this data to add useful content to the site that matches what your potential customers are looking for, and not just include text that matches keyword strings.

Meeting Your Business Goals

Now we have a list of ideas about how to position and expand our business offerings and have gained insight into our target audience. Next, we want to focus on those areas that will bring us the highest rate of conversion.

This data is easier to obtain if your site is already running. You can use your analytics data and paid search data to find out what is attracting the most attention and what topics attract visitors who are most likely to convert.

Pinpointing conversion is tricky though, since it's based on not only attracting qualified visitors who are searching for the right things, but also on how well the content is positioned on the page and how effective the call to action is. We'll talk more about those components of the funnel in Chapter 4. For now, just know that the numbers you see in your web analytics program and paid search reports may not tell the whole story.

Using Web Analytics Data

You can categorize web analytics data in much the same way as keyword research data. Export the information into Excel, categorize by topic and then discern patterns. We'll talk more about using web analytics data in Chapter 8, but for now, we'll just look at the data that helps us understand how our audience is converting.

For instance, if you use Google Analytics, you can generate information about search queries that brought visitors to your site by choosing Traffic Sources > Keywords > Unpaid.

We'll cluster all of the branded searches (that is, searches for our brand name or domain name) together and exclude them, as those searching specifically for us should convert at a higher rate. And we'll exclude queries that clearly aren't targeted for our business. These will be fairly easy to recognize, as they'll have little relevance to your core business. For instance, untargeted queries for our B&B may include [where to buy Napa Valley brand clothing in Rhode Island], [Napa Auto Parts], and [San Diego B&B].

We may find good engagement from people searching for wine-related information, but poor engagement from those searching more generally for things to do. From this, we can decide to either concentrate on adding wine-related information or evaluating the section of the site that focuses on things to do to ensure it is compelling and has a strong call to action.

By default, web analytics data generally only capture things like visits, time on site, number of pages visited, and bounce rate (the percentage of visitors who abandoned the site immediately). For better insight, you'll want to have your analytics team add conversion tracking. With conversion tracking, you specify what constitutes a conversion (in the case of our B&B, this may be completing an online reservation form or sending a message via the contact form) and can then track this across search queries.

Using Paid Search Data

If you run paid search campaigns, you can use this data for better insight into your potential customers as well. And if you don't run paid search campaigns, you might consider running a small one just to gather data

Keyword	Average Pos	Impressions	Clicks	CTR	Conversion Rate %	Average CPC	CPA
sonoma bed and breakfast	1.4	396,797	13,415	3.38%	10.53%	$1.08	$10.25
sonoma inn	1.3	371,257	12,213	3.29%	9.14%	$0.94	$10.32
sonoma lodging	1.2	74,532	5,759	7.73%	9.15%	$0.83	$9.07
sonoma hotels	1.5	25,695	1,433	5.58%	12.07%	$0.62	$5.13
napa valley b b	1.8	10,112	793	7.84%	11.48%	$0.90	$7.88
sonoma chamber of commerce	1.3	14,988	752	5.02%	9.44%	$0.60	$6.31
sonoma resorts	1.4	103,643	923	0.89%	7.80%	$0.46	$5.94

Figure 2.13   Using Paid Search Data for Search Insights

Source: Personal Screenshot

on how potential customers react to the ads and resulting landing pages before investing a lot of resources building out that content.

Your paid search data should look something like this and include information such as average ad position, number of impressions, number of clicks, resulting click through rate (CTR), number of conversions and conversion rate (see Figure 2.13).

So, for instance, you may run two ads that result in the AdWords comparison as shown in Figure 2.14.

From this, you can see that 36 percent of searchers who saw your "Napa Valley B&B" ad clicked through to the site, and nearly 3 percent of those visitors booked a room (or filled out a request for information form or performed any other action you've set up as a conversion event). On the other hand, only 12 percent of those who saw your "wine country lodging" ad clicked through to the site, but once there, nearly 4.5 percent of those visitors converted. Which is the better audience? We can discern the following:

- More people are likely searching for the phrase "Napa Valley B&B" than for "wine country lodging" since that ad has considerably more impressions.

	A	B	C	D	E	F	G
1	Query	Ad Position	Impressions	Clicks	CTR	Conversions	Conversion
2	Napa Valley B&B	2	5,253	1,880	36%	56	2.98%
3	Wine country lodging	1	3,617	450	12%	20	4.44%

Figure 2.14   Using AdWords to Compare Searcher Behavior

Source: Google AdWords

- A higher percentage of searchers are clicking on the Napa Valley ad, but a higher percentage of wine country searchers are converting. What does each ad look like? Is the Napa Valley ad substantially more compelling?
- Since the wine country searchers are converting at a higher rate, they are worth seeking out. What related terms are they searching for? (wine country B&B? wine country inns?)
- The Napa Valley searchers are converting at a lower rate. Is this because, as a group, they aren't quite as qualified, or is it because the page is geared towards the wine country group? Does the page talk about wine country lodging but not about Napa Valley B&Bs? It may be a good idea to implement A/B testing to try out different versions of the page that cause the Napa Valley group to convert at a higher rate, while not driving down the conversion rate of the wine country group.
- As a data source for organic search keyword research, it's likely worth catering to both of these groups and you can likely modify the pages in a way that benefits both paid and organic search traffic and conversions.

You can also use other business data to formulate a more complete picture. What do offline sales look like? Direct mail? E-mail campaigns? What press releases picked up the most interest?

Competitive Research

We've already seen some competitive research with the data available from the Google AdWords Keyword Tool. Let's take a closer look. In the tool, competitive information shows up as a bar graph, and when you export the information, it shows up as a number between 0 and 1. Since this data is based on the competition for paid search terms, it may not correlate exactly with organic search, but it can provide a pretty good gauge to start from.

For instance, consider the following four queries, which have about the same query volume each month (see Figure 2.15).

We can see that, about the same number of people search for each of these per month, but [winery Napa] has much lower competition than the others. If we ran a Northern California winery and were wondering

Query	Volume	Competition
napa wineries	74,123	0.73
sonoma hotels	73,831	0.93
sonoma wine	74,213	0.80
winery napa	74,021	0.46

Figure 2.15   Query Competition
Source: Google AdWords

how best to craft our Web site messaging, we may want to go with the terms with lower competition, as it may be easier to rank for those terms.

We can also use Google trends and keyword data for insight into particular competitors (see Figure 2.16).

Other types of competitive research are available. We'll look at a few below. A more comprehensive list of tools is available at marketing intheageofgoogle.com.

Site Comparison and Traffic Tools

A number of tools exist that compare sites and provide traffic estimates for them. While these tools provide adequate comparisons and good

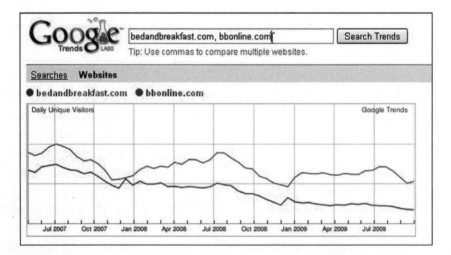

Figure 2.16   Using Google Trends to Compare Web sites
Source: Google Trends

insight into relative changes over time, don't put too much faith in the absolute numbers. Because of the different data collection methods and estimation processes, the exact numbers are, at best, wildly inaccurate.

Compete[14] provides data about the top keywords that are sending searchers to a particular site (see Figure 2.17).

SpyFu[15] provides organic and paid search data about any Web site (see Figure 2.18).

Google Trends for Web sites[16] enables you to compare the traffic trends of multiple Web sites (see Figure 2.19).

Alexa[17] gathers data from its toolbar users and makes available trends data, comparative information, and keyword data, among other things (see Figures 2.20 and 2.21).

Figure 2.17   Compete as Comparison and Traffic Tool

Source: Compete.com

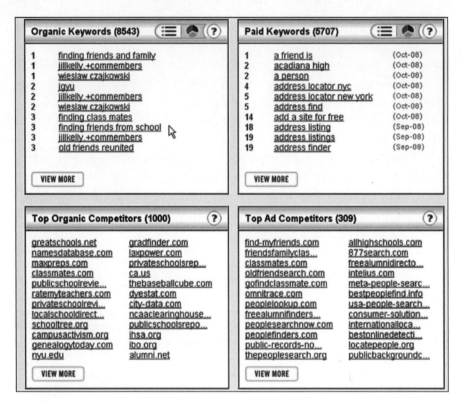

Figure 2.18   Spyfu as Comparison and Traffic Tool
Source: Spyfu.com

One particularly interesting data point is the list of sites that users visit directly before the site in question. For instance, with Olympus .com, we see that over 36 percent came from parent Olympus sites, olympusamerica.com and olympus-global.com, and close to 20 percent came from search engines Google and Yahoo! (see Figure 2.22).

Digging further, we find that over 42 percent of visitors to olympus america.com came from major search engines such as Google and Yahoo! (see Figure 2.23).

Consider the customer base Olympus could be losing if it didn't appear in search results.

Hitwise[18] data comes from partnerships with internet service providers that log the sites their users visit and what they search for. Hitwise products are paid services that include competitive analysis, keyword

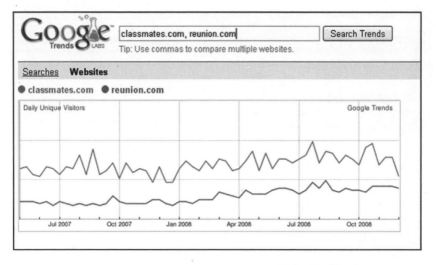

Figure 2.19   Google Trends as Comparison and Traffic Tool

Source: Google Trends

Figure 2.20   Alexa as Comparison and Traffic Tool

Source: Alexa.com

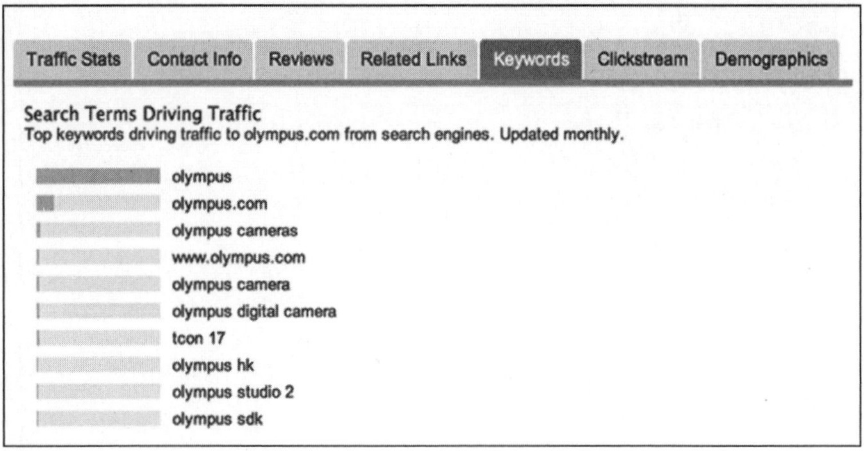

| Traffic Stats | Contact Info | Reviews | Related Links | Keywords | Clickstream | Demographics |

Search Terms Driving Traffic
Top keywords driving traffic to olympus.com from search engines. Updated monthly.

olympus
olympus.com
olympus cameras
www.olympus.com
olympus camera
olympus digital camera
tcon 17
olympus hk
olympus studio 2
olympus sdk

Figure 2.21   Search Terms Driving Traffic for Olympus
Source: Alexa.com

research, clickstream reporting, and demographic information. It also provides free industry reports (see Figures 2.24 and 2.25).

ComScore[19] provides panel-based research, and like Hitwise, produces industry reports and offers fee-based services. Its products include

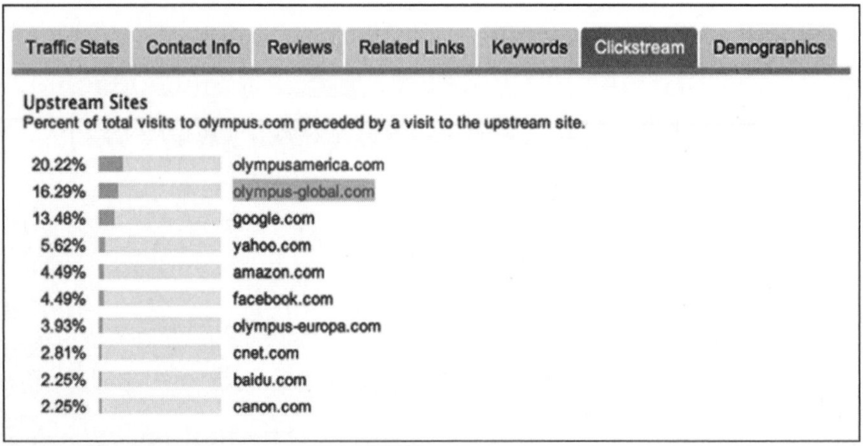

| Traffic Stats | Contact Info | Reviews | Related Links | Keywords | Clickstream | Demographics |

Upstream Sites
Percent of total visits to olympus.com preceded by a visit to the upstream site.

20.22%	olympusamerica.com
16.29%	olympus-global.com
13.48%	google.com
5.62%	yahoo.com
4.49%	amazon.com
4.49%	facebook.com
3.93%	olympus-europa.com
2.81%	cnet.com
2.25%	baidu.com
2.25%	canon.com

Figure 2.22   Traffic Sources for Olympus.com
Source: Alexa.com

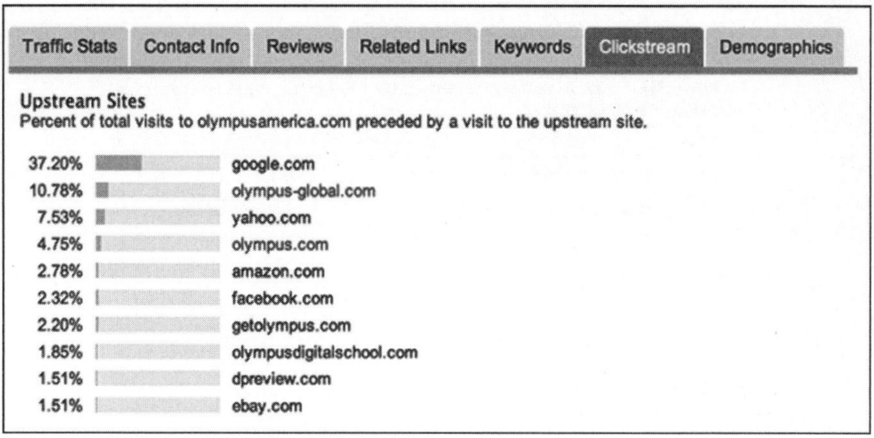

Traffic Stats	Contact Info	Reviews	Related Links	Keywords	Clickstream	Demographics

Upstream Sites
Percent of total visits to olympusamerica.com preceded by a visit to the upstream site.

Percent	Site
37.20%	google.com
10.78%	olympus-global.com
7.53%	yahoo.com
4.75%	olympus.com
2.78%	amazon.com
2.32%	facebook.com
2.20%	getolympus.com
1.85%	olympusdigitalschool.com
1.51%	dpreview.com
1.51%	ebay.com

Figure 2.23   Traffic Sources for Olympusamerica.com

Source: Alexa.com

Top 10 Retail Search Terms

The following report shows **search terms** for the industry **'Shopping and Classifieds'**, ranked by **Clicks** for the **4 weeks** ending **09/12/2009**.

Rank	Search Term	Clicks
1.	craigslist	4.62%
2.	ebay	2.51%
3.	craigslist.com	0.54%
4.	craigs list	0.54%
5.	walmart	0.50%
6.	ebay.com	0.49%
7.	amazon	0.48%
8.	netflix	0.30%
9.	www.craigslist.com	0.29%
10.	amazon.com	0.29%

Figure 2.24   Top 10 Retail Search Terms from Hitwise

Source: Hitwise.com

Top Institutions Search Terms

The following report shows **search terms** for the industry **'Education - Institutions'**, ranked by **Clicks** for the **4 weeks** ending **09/12/2009**.

Rank	Search Term	Clicks	
1.	university of phoenix	0.92%	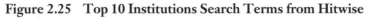
2.	axiaecampus.phoenix.edu	0.48%	
3.	ecampus.phoenix.edu	0.24%	
4.	kaplan university login	0.23%	
5.	ashford university	0.21%	
6.	axia college	0.16%	
7.	devryu.net	0.12%	
8.	troy university	0.12%	
9.	penn foster	0.11%	
10.	mla format	0.11%	

Figure 2.25   Top 10 Institutions Search Terms from Hitwise

Source: Hitwise.com

comScore Marketer, which provides search market share, audience, and analytics analysis, and comScore qSearch, which reports on searcher behavior and activity across the web (not just at major search engines) (see Figure 2.26).

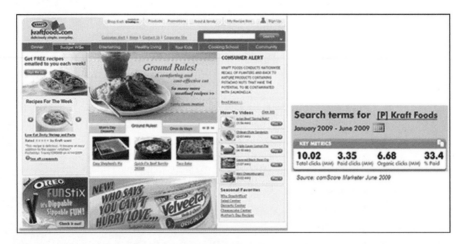

Figure 2.26   Kraftfoods.com comScore Data

Source: ComScore.com

Nielsen NetRatings[20] also provides panel research—an extension of its television panel research—and provides both free and paid reports on searcher behavior and keyword volumes.

You can also simply look at competitors' Web sites. What terms do they use on their pages? Does their site cover additional topics? What sites link to them?

Using Search Results for Competitive Intelligence

A wealth of data is available from simply looking at the search results. When you search for the queries you're targeting, you can see exactly what sites the search engines think are the most relevant for those queries, and how they stack up. You don't know, of course, what the conversion data is like for those sites, but you can click over and see what the searcher workflow experience is like. (We'll be discussing the searcher workflow experience more in Chapter 4.) Look, for instance, at the search results for [accounting software] (see Figure 2.27).

The related searches tell us that many searchers are looking for Microsoft accounting software, so they are clearly a top-of-mind brand for potential customers. The top three brands Google lists in results are QuickBooks, Peachtree, and Sage. Those are the primary brands you'll be competing with in search and in brand mindshare among searchers.

Looking at those top three pages that rank organically, we can see that the QuickBooks page has a compelling value proposition and clear call to action, although some potential customers might not be initially ready to sign up right away and would be more effectively engaged with a larger "learn more" link (see Figure 2.28).

Peachtree does a better job with inviting visitors to learn more, but centers its value proposition on a low price, rather than compelling features (see Figure 2.29).

The Sage site makes its software seem complicated and not necessarily even accounting-related. My eye is drawn to the "what's the right software for me" wizard, which only reinforces my sense of complexity (see Figure 2.30).

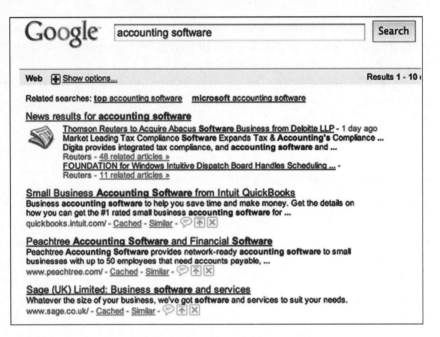

Figure 2.27   Google Search Results: [Accounting Software]
Source: Google Search Results

Figure 2.28   QuickBook's Compelling Value Proposition
Source: Intuit

Figure 2.29   Sage Peachtree Focuses on Price
Source: Peachtree

When I click on the related search [top accounting software], I see that the results primarily focus on the comparison of articles rather than brands, which means ranking a brand site for that query would likely be difficult. (The same is true of the [accounting software lists] and [types of accounting software] related searches at the bottom of the page.) However the related searches [simple accounting software], [bookkeeping

Figure 2.30   Sage's General Site Introduces Complexity
Source: Sage

software], and [personal accounting software] all bring up brand results, so those are good initial targets.

A Better Strategy for Increased Customers and a More Successful Business

Once you've got a sense of the types of things your target audience is interested in the most and how competitive those markets are, you can consider the impact on your business in a number of ways:

- **Product strategy:** Are you providing the types of things your audience is looking for? Are you investing resources in areas that your audience isn't interested in at the expense of areas that it is? If you identify gaps between your product offering and what you find your audience is interested in based on search data, you may want to spend a bit more time asking your customers, setting up focus groups, or analyzing spending patterns.
- **Business strategy:** Is your industry in decline or a state of growth? Are you using the best revenue model for your business? Or are you trying to sell everyone new home loans when they're looking for mortgage refinance?
- **Search acquisition strategy:** What audience and interests lead to the highest conversion rates? What audience is large enough without overwhelming competition? What search terms should you target and what kind of experience should you make available on the site? This process is very similar to the ways you can use this data when building your product and business strategies.

You already know how to use data effectively to improve your product and business strategies, but what about your organic search strategy? The key is to understand the search acquisition workflow: Focus on the searchers, what they are looking for, how you can meet their needs, and how you can compel them to meet your business goals.

We'll learn more about developing a search acquisition strategy in the next few chapters.

Chapter 2 Checklist: Using Search Data

Identify your business goals:

- [ ] What's the primary goal of the business?
- [ ] How will you measure success?
- [ ] What is the primary goal of the Web site?
- [ ] Identify your target audience: Who are they? What are they trying to accomplish?
- [ ] What are the general industry trends based on external search data?
    Use Google Trends to see search volume trends for relevant queries across regions.
- [ ] What core topics is the primary audience most interested in?
    Use the Google AdWords Keyword tool to determine highest-interest topics.
    Use web analytics data and other internal data in conjunction with external search data.
    Use web analytics data to determine how most visitors are finding the site.
    Use web analytics referral data to determine the pages that bring in the most traffic through links.
- [ ] Of the high-interest topics, which intersect with business goals?
    Use web analytics data, paid search data, business goals, and conversion data from other departments to isolate a subset of topics that attract the most qualified potential customers.
- [ ] Which topics align with brand messaging, product plans, and overall strategy?
- [ ] Do any of these topics indicate that product plans and business goals should be revisited?
- [ ] What is the competitive landscape?
    Use tools such as Google Trends for Web sites, Compete, and Hitwise to better understand the competition.
    Use data for audience analysis.

(continued)

(continued)

- [ ] Which audience needs are not being met that your business can capitalize on?
- [ ] Who is your audience?
- [ ] Now that you've identified a subset of topics to focus on, who is this audience and what is it really looking for?

CHAPTER

How We Search

The search acquisition funnel begins with understanding the searcher. Searchers themselves provide very little that indicates their intent. Search queries are an average of three words long and nearly 25 percent are only one word.[1]

Fortunately, we have a great deal of data beyond the queries themselves to help us derive potential intent. Search engines track searcher behavior and by looking at what searchers click on and what they search for next, search engines can learn a great deal about what someone might mean by those one to three words.

We can see much of what the search engines have learned just by looking at what content search engines rank highly for a particular query.

As we've learned, search engines also make a great deal of search data, demographic data, and psychographic data available that can provide detailed insight into the intent and motivation of potential customers.

Query Types

One way search engines derive intent is by classifying queries into intention categories. Each search engine group queries slightly differently, but for our purposes, a good classification system is:

- **Navigational**—With this type of query, the searcher is looking for something specific. These are often one word queries that have a high likelihood of a single meaning. Many, but not all, navigational queries are branded. Some examples are [Volvo] [amazon.com] and [Twitter Vanessa fox]. Approximately 18 percent of search queries are navigational.[2]
- **Commercial (also called transactional)**—These searches are likely purchase-related and the search engines tend to favor results that enable the searcher to buy something, such as e-commerce sites. Some examples of this type of search include [buy shoes online] and [book vacation rental in Greece].
- **Informational (also called research)**—This query tends to be more generic and non-commercial. Search engines tend to favor results that are not commercial in nature. Examples include "when was Abraham Lincoln born" and "highest mountain in the world."
- **Prepurchase research**—For our purposes, it's useful to consider this subset of informational queries in which the searcher is doing research with a high likelihood of a later purchase. Some examples of this type of search include "digital camera reviews" and "what cars get the best gas mileage." This category of searchers is useful to seek out because it's an audience who is not yet ready to purchase but will be soon and is currently gathering data to make decisions about what to buy. You want to provide information to these searchers so they later include you in their list of purchase choices.
- **Action**—This type of query signals that the searcher wants to do something, such as download an application or watch a video. I performed an action query just yesterday when riding in the car with my five-year-old niece. Results for [funny cat videos] on a mobile phone browser can provide hours of entertainment. This type of search can be considered a subset of informational queries.

As noted, search engines determine intent in part based on past search behavior. Search engines see millions of searches a day, and, over a period of years, this data can be very valuable in determining likely intent.

For instance, if one million people a day search for [Britney Spears] and 80 percent of those searchers clicked on a search result that linked to a video or did a second search for [Britney Spears video] (called query refinement), then the search engine looking at this data might conclude that generally, searchers looking for Britney Spears are actually looking for Britney Spears videos. To provide the most useful results for those searchers, the search engine might start surfacing videos in the search results even though the query alone didn't indicate that desire.

How is this useful to you? If you run a Britney Spears site, you can increase your coverage by adding videos to your site so your site has the opportunity to rank not only for the Web page, but for videos as well.

Determining Intent

Most searches are short because of what economist and psychologist Herbert Simon called "bounded rationality."[3] We exert the smallest effort (short queries) to get an adequate result. We only exert more effort (query refinement) if the initial work didn't get us what we needed.

Google's quality guidelines give an example of how difficult it can be to determine intent from a single-word query:

Someone searching for [calendar] could be looking to find and print a calendar for the current month. Or they could be looking for a calendar of holidays. Or they could be looking for an online calendar to use for appointments.

Google breaks the query interpretation into three categories:

- Dominant interpretation
- Common interpretations
- Minor interpretations

Some of the factors that Google uses to determine intent include:

- **Current events**—the searcher likely wants the latest of something (such as latest sports scores versus historical ones).

- **Location**—if the query is regional in nature but doesn't include a location, the searcher likely is interested in their current location (such as local pizza restaurants versus national ones).
- **Previous behavior**—Google uses both overall searcher behavior in aggregate and individual searcher behavior to predict current intent.

Intent factors heavily into how search results are generated globally and in personalized results (discussed on page 117).

The easiest way to find out what search engines have learned about searcher intent is to conduct searches and evaluate the results. Take the query [iPod Touch], for instance. The results include not only the official Apple site and sites that describe the iPod Touch, but also video results, news results, and shopping results (see Figure 3.1).

These results are a clear indication that many searching for [iPod Touch] went on to view videos, news, and e-commerce sites. The suggested related searches tell us that many did subsequent searches for the third generation iPod Touch and the model with a camera.

Query Refinements

Query refinements are the queries searchers type in after doing an initial search. They might do these refinements right away (without clicking on results) or after visiting a few pages and then returning to the search engine. Searchers often enter refinements when the initial search doesn't provide satisfactory results, but the results do provide clues on what to search for.[4]

For instance, if someone does a search for a high school name and gets a set of results with that high school name, but not the correct one, the searcher might notice that the results that appear have geographic information and add that to the query. [South High School] (in Bakersfield, CA), might refine to [South High School Bakersfield CA].

Why do searchers refine their queries? An August, 2009 Hitwise study about Canadian searchers found that searches were successfully

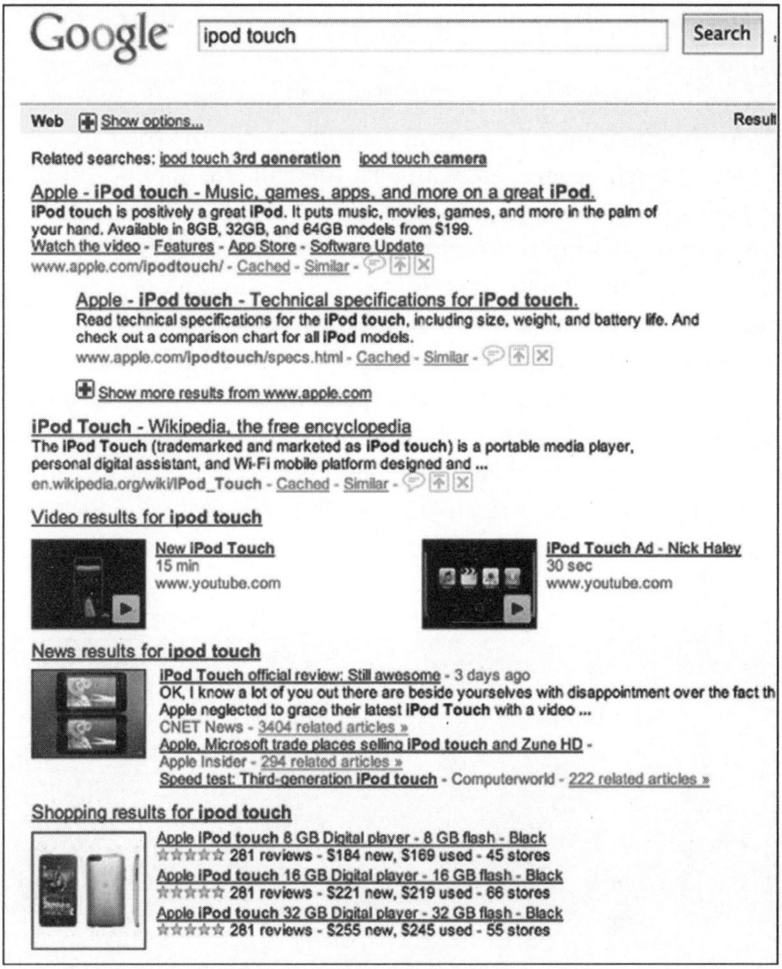

Figure 3.1   Google Search Results: [iPod Touch]
Source: Google Search Results

only 70 percent of the time and the rest of the time searchers had to "re-search to find relevant results."[5]

In this particular study, Hitwise found that the lack of relevance might stem from the international nature of the searches. Since the searches were conducted in North America in English, search engines seemed to weigh U.S. sites more heavily. So, for instance, a search for a particular retail store in Canada might produce results for U.S. store locations.

A Penn State researcher found that 22 percent of queries are refined. At the beginning of a search, searchers narrow their queries and then as the search progresses, searchers reformulate queries (often based on what results appear).

A Microsoft Bing internal study found that searchers refine their queries, bounce back to the search results, or abandon the search 50 percent of the time. The breakdown of that 50 percent is shown in Figure 3.2.

Microsoft also found that searchers repeated 24 percent of their queries during a session. Forty-one percent of searchers change their search term (or search engine) if they don't find what they're looking for on the first page of results, and 88 percent do so after three pages.[6]

During information retrieval, searchers often change focus to different aspects of their tasks.[7] This change may cause searchers to refine

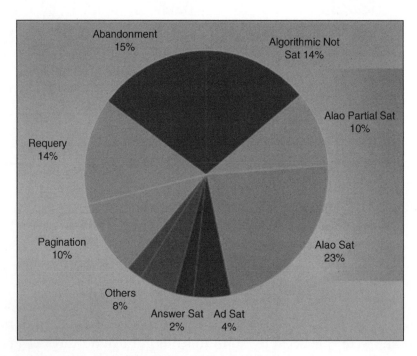

Figure 3.2   Microsoft Bing Internal Study Results
Source: Bing

their queries to broader or narrower concepts, from topical to non-topical searches, and to unexpected shifts.

The search engines try to help searchers narrow in on what they're looking for and to provide refinement suggestions in a number of ways.

It can be valuable to make note of what refinements the engines suggest, both because it sheds light on what searchers are likely looking for (since refinements tend to be based on past search behavior) and because searchers will often choose the refinement in the initial search. It may be difficult to rank for the initial term due to a lot of competition, but you might be able to more easily rank for the longer term.

- **Google search suggest:** Google provides refinement suggestions as the searcher is typing. For a company that sells used cars online, it may be helpful to know that when someone searches for [cars], Google suggests sports cars, old cars, used cars, and cars for sale. The company may have included information on their site about used cars, but perhaps didn't think about mentioning "old" cars (see Figure 3.3).
- **Google related searches:** Google's related searches can also help businesses understand their audience and ensure they can be found for relevant searches. Again, with [cars], we see that Google is suggesting [old cars] as a follow up search, so chances are good that a lot of people looking to buy a used car will click on the old cars link, so you want to make sure that your used car site ranks highly for that search (see Figure 3.4).

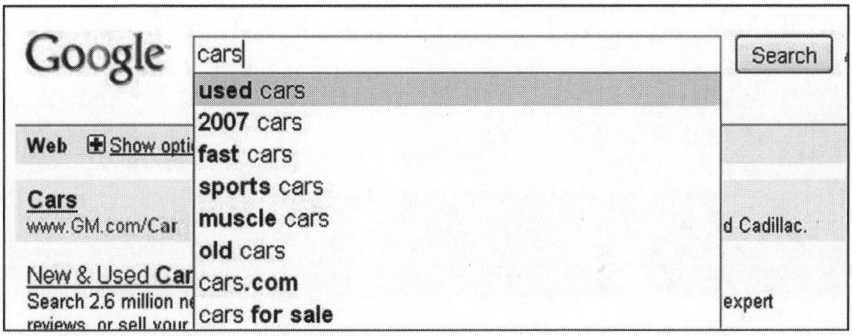

Figure 3.3 Google Search Suggest: [Cars]
Source: Google

> Searches related to: **cars**
>
> electric cars   sports cars   old cars   disney cars
>
> cars pixar   car pictures   autotrader   car games

Figure 3.4   Google Related Searches: [Cars]

Source: Google

Figure 3.5   Yahoo! Search Suggestions: [Cars]

Source: Yahoo!

- **Yahoo! search suggestions:** Yahoo! provides a similar set of suggestions in their search box (see Figure 3.5).
- **Yahoo! search assist:** Yahoo! also provides a way for searchers to browse related concepts. This "search assist" feature combines search and browse to help searchers who might otherwise type in just one or two words. The related concepts listed here can provide great insight into searcher intent (see Figure 3.6).
- **Bing categorized search:** Microsoft Bing's categorized search results go one step farther. Not only do the search results suggest refinements, but the page is also broken up into listings for each of them. So a search for [used cars] will not only produce results

Figure 3.6   Yahoo! Search Assist: [Cars]

Source: Yahoo!

Figure 3.7 Bing Categorized Search: [Used Cars]

Source: Bing

for that search, but it will also list results for [local used cars], [prices used cars] and so on. A savvy used car business will want to rank highly for each of those searches (see Figure 3.7).

Using Demographic Data

Microsoft adCenter provides demographic information about searchers based on the search patterns of MSN users. For instance, when looking at shoe searches, we see that 75 percent of searches for [Payless shoes] are from women, whereas men and women search for [running shoes] in nearly equal numbers (with the 25–35 age group searching the most at over 28 percent).

If we combine search volume and gender data, we can generate a shoe-related top 10 keyword list for both men and women (see Figures 3.8 and 3.9). By volume, the top three shoe-related terms men search for are [running shoes], [Jordan shoes], and [Nike shoes]; the top three shoe-related terms women search for are [Payless shoes], [running shoes] and [DSW shoes].

This information could be highly useful to Nike. Their site currently isn't on the first page of Google search results for [running shoes] (see Figure 3.10). The top results are runningshoes.com, roadrunner sports.com, runningwarehouse.com, runnersworld.com, and holabird sports.com. Their competitors Saucony, Brooks, and New Balance do rank on the first page, and the first Nike-related result is a site called bestbuynike.com.

Women Top 10 (Weighted by Volume)		
Keyword	% Female	W
payless shoes	74.26%	
running shoes	48.25%	
dsw shoes	74.77%	
nike shoes	52.94%	
jordan shoes	45.14%	
bakers shoes	77.38%	
aldo shoes	75.66%	

Figure 3.8   Demographic Information: Searching for Women's Shoes
Source: Microsoft adCenter

In July 2009, 1,830,000 people searched Google for running shoes. Nike would probably like a share of those searchers.

If searches for your product are done primarily by one gender, consider how they process language and shop differently. Researchers from Northwestern University and the University of Haifa found that the areas of the brain associated with language work harder in girls than in boys. So, perhaps copy aimed at men should be succinct and to the point.

In *Why We Buy: The Science of Shopping*, Paco Underhill noted that fewer men look for price tags.[8] And some research has found that men are more likely to make impulse purchases online. You can incorporate this data into other audience analysis and market research that you have and may decide that your product pages aimed at women should have highly visible prices and ensure information that answers questions is easily available.[9]

Men Top 10 (Weighted by Volume)		
Keyword	% Male	W
running shoes	51.75%	
jordan shoes	54.86%	
nike shoes	47.06%	
payless shoes	25.74%	
dc shoes	51.84%	

Figure 3.9   Demographic Information: Searching for Men's Shoes
Source: Microsoft adCenter

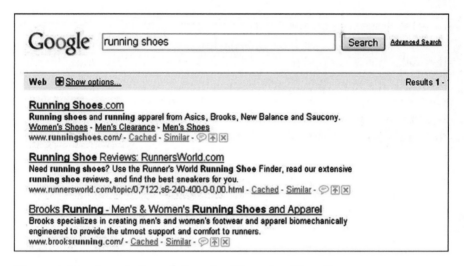

Figure 3.10   Google Search Results: [Running Shoes]
Source: Google Search Results

Studies have also shown that online, women are more engaged with images and men are less patient. This means that men are more likely to abandon your home page if it starts loading a Flash module. Men are also more impatient with poor navigational structure.

A study that focused on differences in how men and women search found that "on average, men make decisions quicker, spend less time on sites, are more likely to have preestablished 'favored' vendor sites that they use in the search process and show less resistance to sponsored listings. Women tended to be more deliberate in reading search results, spend more time with their searches and spend more time on sites before making decisions."[10]

Consider the age of your target audience as well. If you cater to an older audience, make sure that when they click the search results to your site, the type is larger and clear and easy to read.

How Searchers Interact with Results

Gord Hotchkiss, CEO of Enquiro Research, has given us fascinating insight into the way searchers view and click on results.

He describes how our brains use cognitive shortcuts when performing mental tasks. As we learn a behavior, we internalize it and perform that behavior on autopilot so our brains are free to concentrate on other tasks. Up to 45 percent of our daily actions are done by habit, without conscious thought.[11] Our brains take similar shortcuts when scanning the search results page. We don't initially read the text on the page; we look for matches in the shape of the characters in the query. Hotchkiss notes:

> *In cognitive psychology, this is called the "pop out" effect. We can recognize shapes much faster than we can read words. The shapes of our query literally "pop out" from the page as a first step toward matching relevance. The effect is enhanced by query (or hit) bolding. This matching game is done at the sub-cortical level.[12]*

How Working Memory Plays into Evaluating Search Results

Enquiro's eye tracking studies have shown that we scan the page in an F-shaped pattern: we start in the upper left and then move down the left margin (see Figure 3.11).

Because of the capacity of our working memory, we break the page into chunks of three to four results. This corresponds to cognitive psychologist George Miller's rule of "7 +/− 2," which posits that our working memory can hold around seven chunks of information.[13] We can hold more digits than words in our working memory, which may partially explain how we evaluate search results. A 2008 study at UC Davis found that our working memory only allows us to consider three to four things at one time.[14]

Rather than evaluate all results on the page at once, we first evaluate a single three to four item chunk and move on to the next if we don't find a match. Fifty percent of the time, searchers click on results in the first chunk.

This is one reason why a number one ranking is less important than people think. If you rank in the top three to four results and have the most compelling title and description, you may win the click over the sites ranking above you.

Why don't we feel compelled to review the results in all of the chunks before making a decision? It likely has to do, once again, with

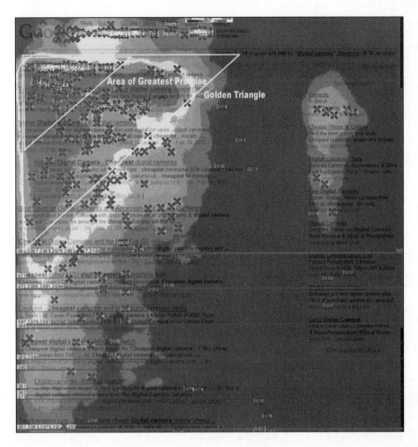

Figure 3.11   Eye Tracking Heat Map of Search Results

Source: Enquiro

bounded rationality. If we reach an adequate solution within the first chunk, we have no reason to continue our evaluation.

All of this chunking and scanning takes place in milliseconds. Once we see a positive pattern match in a result, our eyes rest on that result long enough to read the words. When we see words that reinforce that this result is relevant for the query (we may recognize the brand) or see a description includes positive attributes we were looking for but didn't include in the query (such as a regional location or price attribute), we may click.

One Enquiro study involved finding out if searchers with different intents (commercial versus information gathering) scanned results differently. They showed both groups the same set of algorithmic and sponsored results. They found that both groups scanned the results in nearly the same way. The difference happened at the click. In the commercial intent group, half of the searchers clicked the algorithmic results and half clicked the paid search results. In the information gathering group, everyone clicked the algorithmic results. This happened even though both groups looked at the algorithmic and paid search results in exactly the same way and for the same amount of time.[15]

Our search autopilot only switches off once we are ready to click on a result. The entire interaction generally takes less than ten seconds. We spend less than two seconds evaluating each result before the click.

So if we scan results a chunk at a time and evaluate each cluster of results, what are we evaluating? What is displayed in that result can make a big difference in whether that listing gets a click.

What Compels a Click?

We subconsciously look for relevancy clues in the title and snippet once we've paused on a result. For instance, if we're looking for a car, we might respond positively to words like "fuel efficient" and "5 star crash rating."

Some businesses don't like seeing their competition rank highly in the results along with them. But this might not be such a bad thing. One study found that when a well-known competitor was missing from results, searchers found the results to be less trustworthy and didn't feel as comfortable clicking.[16]

How Important Is a Number One Ranking?

As we discovered earlier, if your search result is more compelling than those around it, searchers may very well click on it if it's within the cluster they're evaluating, even if it isn't ranked highest. But ranking well does make a difference. Sixty-two percent of searchers click a result on the first page of results and 90 percent click within the first three pages.[17] Data leaked from AOL shows that first page rankings are even more important, as 90 percent of clicks within that data set were on the first page of results.[18]

Breakdown of the Search Results Page

According to a study by Bernard J. Jansen at Penn State University, 60 percent of searchers rely primarily on the title of the result when evaluating whether to click.[19]

And as we saw earlier in the eye tracking heat maps, searchers don't even evaluate the entire title—they look primarily at the left half of it. The description displayed under the title and the URL also factor into what a searcher clicks on. Search engines bold words in all three places that match the query, which can draw a searcher's attention.

In the search results below for the query [rheumatoid arthritis], searchers may skip the second result when scanning, since the words that match the query don't appear in the left side of the title (see Figure 3.12).

Many businesses don't think about optimizing the description listed under the title of their search results, but that is your one opportunity to provide a compelling marketing message and entice potential customers to click. We'll take a closer look at these descriptions on page 165.

Even worse than not optimizing the title and description of your listing is not providing them at all. For instance, see the search results display of some high profile brands that have spent considerable ad dollars on offline campaigns that have spurred search volume.

Figure 3.12   Analyzing Search Snippets

Source: Google Search Results

Figure 3.13   Poor Search Results Display
Source: Google Search Results

    With this Sprint listing, for instance, no description appears and the title is less than helpful (see Figure 3.13).

    And here, the text that compels searchers to click is from an Atlas tracking code (see Figure 3.14).

    Verizon doesn't do much better (see Figure 3.15).

Enhancing Your Results

We can see that descriptive, compelling search results can help motivate a click, and you can take further advantage of how the search engines are evolving the way these results are displayed.

    Yahoo!, for instance, has a program called SearchMonkey that enables Web developers to include additional details such as photos, links, ratings, and store hours to the listing. Google has begun extracting metadata from pages to display similar information with a program it

Figure 3.14   Broken Code Impacting Search Results Display
Source: Google Search Results

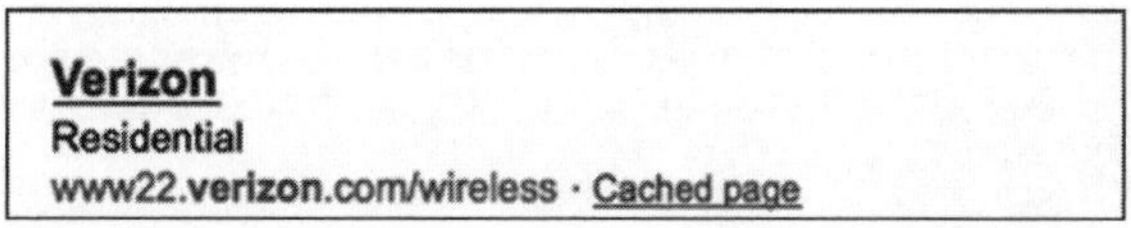

> **Verizon**
> Residential
> www22.**verizon**.com/wireless · Cached page

Figure 3.15   Even Large Brands Can Have Poor Search Results Descriptions

Source: Google Search Results

calls *Rich Snippets*. Bing extracts details from the Web page and displays them in a pop up that appears when the searcher hovers the mouse over the listing.

Amit Kumar, of Yahoo!'s SearchMonkey, states, "Our tests uncovered that users found these [SearchMonkey] apps useful; in fact, in some cases, we saw a lift in click-through rate of as high as 15 percent."[20]

The details of these programs go beyond the scope of this book, but refer to Chapter 7 for suggestions about how you can ensure your Web developers are taking full advantage of these initiatives and see marketingintheageofgoogle.com for additional resources.

How Searchers Evaluate the Page They've Clicked On

We can judge a site visually in as little as 50 milliseconds.[21] And when performing a task, we focus on that and become blind to anything else. Even if visitors to a site look directly at something, they may not see it at all if it doesn't obviously apply to their task.

This behavior correlates well with customer behavior in a store. In *Why We Buy*, Paco Underhill describes how shoppers enter stores. They don't stop at the front door and look around. They walk in and scan as they go. Much of what they see during this transition is lost on them.[22]

Even in physical stores, shoppers scan words quickly. "Putting a sign that requires 12 seconds to read in a place where customers spend four seconds is just slightly more effective than putting it in your garage," says Underhill.

Product placement can help maximize sales both in stores and on your site. The salsa will sell better next to the chips than next to the mustard.

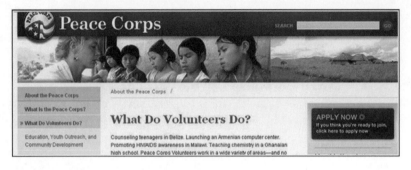

Figure 3.16   Peace Corps Web Site Visitor Experience

Source: Peacecorps.gov

For the purpose of search strategy, it's important to understand that what page the searcher lands on and how easily the searcher can scan the page and recognize that it answers their query is a vital part of the search acquisition funnel.[23]

Consider the query [what do Peace Corps volunteers do]. It leads searchers to a page that clearly answers the searcher's question. The context and purpose of the page are clear on even a quick scan (see Figure 3.16).

From Page to Conversion

Once the searcher lands on your page and confirms the content will satisfy the search, make sure the page will also fulfill the business need and not simply lead to a dead end. In the next chapter, we'll dive into the details of developing searcher personas, which include pinpointing company goals and ensuring that those are presented as clear calls to action on the page. In the case of the Peace Corps example in Figure 3.16, we can see that the page has a clear and obvious call to action with the Apply Now button.

Consider this PEAK6 recruiting page, on the other hand. It not only doesn't provide a clear heading to anchor the visitor about the context of the page, but the primary business purpose for creating the page at all (gathering job applicants) is hidden in a tiny link at the bottom of the page that is easily overlooked (see Figure 3.17).

Figure 3.17   PEAK6's Call to Action Is Unclear
Source: PEAK6.com

See more on how PEAK6 is now using search data to improve their business in the next chapter.

An effective way to intersect searcher interest and business needs to identify key audience segments is by building searcher personas. You can then map out a compelling conversion path for these personas by way of searcher conversion workflows. You can use these workflows to determine key points of collaboration between departments of your organization.

Building Searcher Personas

Opening the Door to the Crowd of Customers
You've Been Keeping Out

By now you have learned how to use search data to improve your overall product and business strategies and seen the value of developing a search acquisition strategy. Next, we'll put these pieces together by using what you've learned about your business and potential customers to create searcher personas and search acquisition workflows that harness the power of search data for opening a whole new channel of acquisition.

Your customers are already looking for what you have to offer, but they often aren't searching specifically for your brand. If your site doesn't appear for their non-branded searches, you could very well fall off their consideration list.

If you're doing offline advertising and not ensuring your brand shows up for the subsequent search traffic that advertising triggers, you may as well be running TV commercials but keeping the store locked up with no way for customers to get in.

Remember those old Mervyn's super sale ads in which the crowds of customers stood outside the closed store chanting, "Open, open, open?" That's exactly what's happening when you don't ensure organic search is a fundamental part of your customer acquisition strategy. Your audience is standing at the door, and you're not letting them in.

Search Acquisition Strategy Process

As you probably realize by now, a successful search acquisition strategy involves more than just someone at the company with the job title of SEO (see Chapter 6 for more details about search engine optimization and how it ties into a successful search strategy). A successful strategy involves:

- Ensuring all business and product goals are aligned and using search data as a key part of market research.
- Identifying a target audience that is most likely to turn into customers.
- Determining the queries that fit your business needs and are conducted by your target audience in significant volumes.
- Building content that not only ranks well for those queries, but provides a user experience that helps searchers complete their tasks and engages them more deeply with your business.
- Offering a call to action that compels the searcher deeper into the conversion funnel.
- Understanding what metrics provide actionable insights into the effectiveness of the strategy.

This process involves the steps below:

- Identify your business goals—
  - → What is the business purpose?
  - → What is the Web site purpose?
- Assess the market opportunity—
  - → Based on keyword research, what searches are relevant to your business?
  - → What's the overall volume?
- Assess the conversion potential—
  - → What queries will drive conversion (based on your business goals)?

$\longrightarrow$ Who is the target audience?

$\longrightarrow$ What's the competitive landscape?

- Create a tactical plan.
- Develop searcher personas.
- Develop search conversion workflows—

$\longrightarrow$ Build a content strategy based on the searcher personas and search conversion workflows.

- Execute the technical implementation (see Chapter 7).
- Monitor progress.
- Identify actionable metrics (see Chapter 8).
- Create rollout and adjustment strategies.

Identify Your Business Goals

It's important to have a clear sense of your business goals in mind as you embark on developing a search strategy because they provide context for using the search data you collect, identifying your target audience segments, and building a conversion workflow that supports those overall goals.

Consider both your primary and secondary business goals. For instance, in the case of the Napa Valley B&B, the primary business goal is to keep the rooms fully booked, but it's also important to book those rooms at a profitable price, to engage with guests so they have a good experience and return often (and tell their friends), and to make as much information available to them as possible in advance to reduce manual overhead (such as providing directions, recommendations, and assistance with booking wine tours).

It's also important to set concrete goals for the Web site. It's not enough to say that the goal of the Web site is to give your business an online presence. That's not a goal that you can measure, nor is it something that can align all of the departments in the organization toward a common purpose. For our B&B, Web site goals might include:

- Generate leads for offline bookings.
- Enable online bookings.
- Provide answers to frequently asked questions from guests.

We can measure these goals using data points such as:

- Increase the number of offline bookings by 10 percent over six months.
- Book 10 bookings online per month.
- Reduce number of phone calls asking for directions by 50 percent.

A great first step in the goal-articulation process is to step way back and remember what your company is all about at the most basic level. Start your goal discussions by remembering why your company exists: What are you trying to do? Who are you trying to do it for?

Based on your goals, you can build searcher personas that identify the key queries and target audiences that will help you reach them.

Assess the Market Opportunity

We've seen in Chapter 2 how to dive into search data to discover who your customers are, what they're looking for, what the overall industry trends are, and what the competitive landscape looks like.

You can use this data to construct an initial set of target searches.

For every category of content on the site now and for every type of new content you plan to introduce, answer these questions. You should have most of the answers based on the research we've just done.

- What are my business goals (and conversion goals)?
- Who in the target audience is most likely to convert?
- What is this target audience searching for?
- What searches are most likely to lead to conversions?
- What content best meets audience needs for those identified searches?
- What information will compel those visitors to convert?

Evaluate Site Pages for Alignment with Content Strategy

Another way of using this information is evaluating the pages currently on the site and any proposed pages. Ask the following questions:

- What are you trying to accomplish with each page?
- Who are you trying to attract?
- What is that audience searching for?
- Will this page satisfy that search?
- Will this page compel the audience to convert?
- What's the call to action?

Assess the Conversion Potential

Based on your business goals, searcher data, and competitive landscape, you can refine the initial list of target searches to subsets that are most likely to convert and that are reasonable areas for your business to initially compete in. For example, [cheap Viagra] searches have high value and volume, but you'll face strong competition if you choose that as your initial market. On the other hand, [pictures of cute bunnies] may have fairly low competition, but there's not much money to be made in bunny photography.

Create a Tactical Plan

Now we've made it to the core of the work. You've identified a core set of searches and have a good understanding of audience and competitive landscape. You know what actions you'd like those searchers to take once they reach your site. The next step is to develop searcher personas and search conversion workflows that will help you build a content strategy. The rest of this chapter dives into searcher personas and search conversion workflows.

Monitor Progress

Search strategy is an iterative process. One of the most powerful aspects of search as an acquisition channel is that you are provided with near real-time feedback about what's working and what's not. (In Chapter 8, I describe how to measure success and monitor actionable metrics for adjustments after launch.)

Creating Searcher Personas

A *persona* is a highly-detailed description of an individual who embodies key goals and behaviors of an important group of target customers.

Typically, a project team will create a set of prioritized personas and use them to drive decisions throughout a design process. Product design personas are built to embody the "differences that make a difference" between the goals and needs of various intended users of a product or service; searcher personas should capture the "differences that make a difference" in the ways target customers search for (and find) the things you are offering.[1]

Product design personas help organizations build products, sites, and services that make sense once the customer or user starts using them; in the case of a Web site, for example, design personas help teams craft the paths visitors take once they arrive. Searcher personas will help you get the visitors to the site in the first place. In effect, they help you begin the user experience design well before the potential customer reaches your site or store and, indeed, before that customer may even have your brand in mind.

Searcher personas also provide snapshots of your potential customers at different phases of the buying cycle. Since searcher personas can describe both a particular searcher demographic (moms who are looking for safe cars that can fit two children and two adults) as well as a potential customer in a particular part of the purchase cycle (preretirement couples who are researching the best places to live once they retire versus those same couples once they have retired and are ready to move), they are flexible constructs that you can modify to best meet your needs.

When developing searcher personas, you generally classify and identify search query categories from the list of queries you've built. For instance, O'Reilly, which produces technical books and conferences, might begin with the following query categories:

- **Navigational/branded queries**—These include variations of the domain and brand, such as [oreilly], [oreilly.com] and [oreilly Web site]. These queries may also include existing brands such as [head first].
- **Code queries**—These are searches for information about coding-related topics. The searcher may be looking for anything that answers the question or may be specifically looking for a book, conference, or forum/blog. In this case, O'Reilly will want to investigate if it makes sense to set up a separate conversion path for

books, conferences, and forums, or if it would serve these searchers better to have a topic landing page ("All About AJAX") that
links to the various components available for that topic (such as
conference, books, forums, and latest blog posts). Queries along
these lines include [Blackberry hacks], [C# design patterns], [C#
cookbook], [iPhone development].

- **Book-specific queries**—These could include writing-related
queries such as [book writing] and [how to write a book].
- **Author searches**—Searches for author names can likely be aggregated into one persona type. It may make sense to build out
author pages with bio information, links to related sites, books
written, and upcoming speaking events.

Next, perform query category analysis. Aggregate the list of queries
for each category, and then determine the market opportunity, search
volume, competition, and conversion potential. This information will
vary for each category and is useful information for later success metrics.
For each query category, assess:

- What are the related keywords for the category?
- What are the highest volume keywords for each category?
- Does the site rank for any of these terms now? If so, which pages?
- What is the intent of these searchers?
- What are the current ranking, bounce rate, number of pages
viewed, and other conversion event metrics?
- What's the competitive analysis for the category?

Tamara Adlin, author of *The Persona Lifecycle: Keeping
People in Mind Throughout Product Design*

To identify the audiences for your query categories, try completing
an "I want/I need" exercise that's used in an ad-hoc persona cre-
ation process I developed with John Pruitt. Gather your team in a
room and hand out sticky notes. Ask everyone to spend a few

(continued)

(continued)

minutes writing a person + situation on each sticky note. For example, the O'Reilly team might create sticky notes like these:

> Coder looking for a code snippet
>
> Professor trying to find the best book to use for his upcoming class
>
> *Wired* reader who remembers an author name from an article she read
>
> Marketer who heard something about a "polar bear book"
>
> Student who needs bibliographic details to include in a paper
>
> Aspiring author wondering who might print his book idea
>
> Etc.

After everyone has written as many stickies as they can think of (typically, each person in the room will come up with at least 20), have everyone cluster the stickies on a large sheet of paper.

To do the clustering, use a different color sticky note and create "I want . . . " or "I need . . . " category labels. In the O'Reilly example, the team might come up with:

> Category: "I need an answer to a question I have right now"
>> Stickies—Coder looking for a code snippet
>> Student who needs bibliographic details to include in a paper
> Category: "I want to find a book I heard about"
>> *Wired* reader who remembers an author name from an article she read
> Category: "I'm interested in learning about publishing"

> Aspiring author wondering who might print his book idea
>
> Etc.
>
> The category labels you come up with can form the foundation for your searcher personas and can be a good way to do the query classification.

Once you have begun to categorize your audience into searcher personas, you can define the audience for each query category by answering the following questions:

- What do you know about this category of searchers?
- What does success look like for them?
- How can you help them accomplish their task?
- What conversion goal applies to them and what is the likelihood of conversion?
- What stage of the buying cycle are they in? Are they researching? Intending to purchase?
- How can you compel them to conversion?
- What is the lifetime value of this searcher? (This last question is a stretch that most companies haven't quite figured out, so if you haven't gotten there yet, don't worry! Just know that it's useful data to compile once you're able to.)

You may end up with something like Figure 4.1.

Creating Searcher Conversion Workflows

Once you've created searcher personas for each query category (and audience type, if applicable), you can turn that information into an optimal searcher conversion workflow. Use the illustration in Figure 4.2 as a guide.

In order for your search acquisition strategy to be effective, all phases of this workflow must be in place.

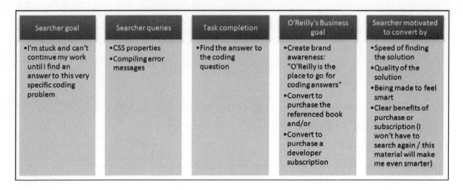

Searcher goal	Searcher queries	Task completion	O'Reilly's Business goal	Searcher motivated to convert by
•I'm stuck and can't continue my work until I find an answer to this very specific coding problem	•CSS properties •Compiling error messages	•Find the answer to the coding question	•Create brand awareness: "O'Reilly is the place to go for coding answers" •Convert to purchase the referenced book and/or •Convert to purchase a developer subscription	•Speed of finding the solution •Quality of the solution •Being made to feel smart •Clear benefits of purchase or subscription (I won't have to search again / this material will make me even smarter)

Figure 4.1   Creating a Searcher Persona

- **Search**—You need to understand your customers and what they're searching for (identified in the searcher persona definitions).
- **Rank**—Your site has to rank well for the identified queries (Chapter 5).
- **SERP (Search Engine Results Page) Display**—The search results display must compel searchers to click through to your site.
- **Page Content**—The page the searcher clicks to should be quickly identifiable as relevant to the searcher's task.
- **Conversion**—The page should propel the visitor to conversion with an effective call to action.

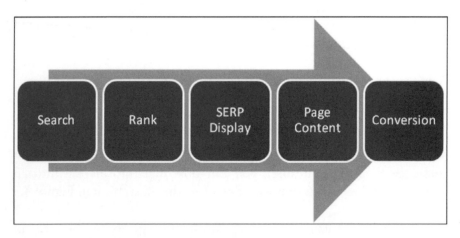

Figure 4.2   Searcher Persona Workflow

Once you've outlined searcher conversion workflows for each searcher persona, you can create a content strategy that takes full advantage of the search opportunity. (You'll learn how best to build this strategy in Chapter 6.)

What Queries to Target

When options brokerage PEAK6 decided to branch out and provide educational information about the stock market to novice investors, they created a virtual trading space that enabled visitors to practice investing with no real money at stake.

Knowing that to learn about the stock market and to invest can be daunting to some (and—sorry brokers!—boring to others), they built WeSeed.com, educational content around topics that got people excited and related those topics to the stock market:

- Excited about that new Apple iPhone? Learn how the release impacted Apple stock.
- Psyched for the next Britney Spears tour? How has it impacted the stock of BMG, her record label?

Sounds great, right? And it is. But they weren't gaining much traction in customer signups. Looking at their Web analytics, it was clear that few visitors were coming from search, even though investment advice is likely a hot search topic.

Two of the areas we looked at were:

How well were the visitors they *were* getting converting to customers?

Was there a different product strategy that would attract more visitors?

We discovered some interesting data in the logs. Most visitors were searching for variations of "virtual stock market" and "stock market game." While this is exactly what We Seed offers, that's not obvious from the pages those searchers were landing on.

Another large subset of searchers was looking for information on teaching their kids to invest, with queries such as [investing for kids] and [stocks for children]. We Seed hadn't considered creating a product that helped teach kids to invest.

We Seed already provided a section for educators, but it was aimed at those teaching at the university level. We considered adding a subsection to the site focused on elementary school teachers—giving them advice, sample games, and educational material they could provide to their students.

We also looked into creating a stock market game that parents could play with their children. Expanding into this product had several advantages. The parents would control the user accounts, so although the kids would be playing, they wouldn't need accounts of their own. We Seed could take advantage of the visitor traffic they were already getting from search and acquire more traffic, which would in turn add activity to the site. And the parents would be introduced to We Seed and the PEAK6 suite of products, which might motivate some of them to sign up for We Seed or PEAK6 accounts.

Determining value to the business is key. A site could build out a number of content and product areas based on search volumes and analytics data. And that would likely add substantial search traffic to the site. But the point behind acquiring search traffic is to convert those visitors to customers. Would building out a section for kids result in conversion?

The process to determine the answer is the same as for any business. Will adding a pool result in the gym seeing more memberships? Will fixing that leaky roof get the house sold quicker?[2]

When I ask business owners what their site goals are, they tell me things like "I want to increase my site traffic by 50 percent" and "I want to rank number one for this particular keyword." But neither of those is a site goal. Those are both steps that can lead to the goal, but neither is the reason behind the site.

In the case of We Seed, conversion goals are hard to pin down. The site doesn't generate revenue—it doesn't sell anything, display ads, or sell memberships. The site simply produces educational content.

Since the site was already getting search traffic for [investing for kids]-related queries without having a targeted product for those visitors (as it ranks on the first page for those queries), odds are that we could vastly increase that traffic fairly easily by focusing on that product strategy.

We also determined that parents who were interested enough in the stock market to want to play an online stock game with their kids that teaches kids investing were a good audience that aligned with the site's goals: increasing awareness of the PEAK6 brand and positioning it as an authoritative thought leader on investment-related advice by providing educational content.

Looking at the competitive landscape, there's room for a better product choice. The top ranking site on Google is called "Investing for Kids," but its content doesn't seem to be targeted for kids, and it appears to be abandoned. It appears to be ranking because the site contains a lot of content and the title of the site matches the query. The next few sites are article-based sites, also mostly abandoned. There don't seem to be any sites that provide easy to use educational content for parents and kids with a game component. Related queries such as [educational games kids investing] list articles from 2001.

By using the Google AdWords Keyword tool, we found that the top three related search queries were:

- Stocks for kids
- Kids stock market
- For kids stock market

None of these queries had significant competition, so the market seemed a good bet for expansion. Looking more closely at the search data, we can begin to paint a more detailed picture of the persona we're targeting. Some searchers want to explain the stock market to kids. Another set of searchers is looking to buy stock *for* their kids, so we decided to exclude it from our targeting. Later, we could expand into educational content around that topic to reach additional searchers.

Next, we did searches for the identified queries to see what the search results would tell us about this audience. Many of the related searches at the bottom of the search results page are about *teaching* kids about the stock market.

WeSeed.com now has data about a potential new target audience, just from looking at search data and their web analytics. So should they drop their current strategy and redirect their business efforts toward kids? Not so fast. Remember, this research also uncovered a key segment of their existing business strategy that they weren't taking advantage of during searches for virtual stock markets and stock market games. Those searchers are a great audience for the existing content on WeSeed.com and are likely highly qualified. We Seed chose to start there and will consider new audiences once they've reached this group who are already searching for exactly what they offer.

But you can see how looking at search data can help you uncover new potential avenues of connecting with an audience and directions your product strategy could go.

Ensuring Each Page Has a Clear and Valuable Call to Action

Every business wants to achieve their goals and they don't want to invest substantial resources on acquiring an audience to whom they don't even offer the chance to convert. But you might be surprised at how easily it can be to overlook the last step in the search conversion workflow—the conversion itself.

To see this in action, let's take a look at PEAK6 again. One of their family sites is Options News Network (onn.tv), a destination for traders to gather insights, news, and analysis around the stock market. They showcase a number of personalities on their site who appear on financial channels such as CNBC. They know that watching television spurs people to search and they want to take advantage of that.

In building individual profile pages for each Options News Network personality, PEAK6 thought about how to best satisfy the needs of searchers as well as meet their business goals. They put together the following goals.

Site Purpose

- Provide self-direct options traders with a single destination that aggregates options news, trade ideas, and content to help people manage risk better.
- Provide options information and education through text and video content.

- Grow the universe of option traders by reaching out to stock investors who will benefit from adding options to their choice of investment tools.

Audience

- Self-directed options traders.
- Stock traders who want to learn about options trading.
- Brokers who are investing on behalf of clients.

The Target Searchers Agenda

- Information on company personalities (such as Jud Pyle) based on seeing them on TV and reading an article about them.
- More details about topic personality discussed. For instance, showing an interest in knowing more about Pyle's opinions on options trading.
- Motivated by:
  - $\longrightarrow$ Credible and comprehensive information.
  - $\longrightarrow$ Compelling content that pulls visitor through mediums to videos, articles, and so on.

Business Goals

- Audience engagement (watch videos, read articles, and comment).
- Site registration.
- Monetization through ads, subscription, or lead generation.

Conversion Metrics

- Return visits.
- Premium memberships.
- Number of videos watched and articles read.

We put together the following searcher persona workflow as shown in Figure 4.3.

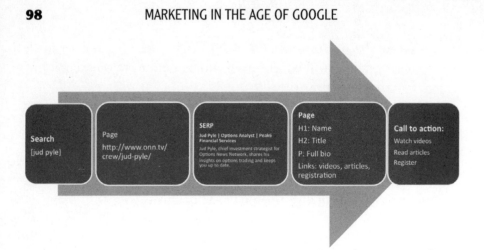

Figure 4.3   [Jud Pyle] Searcher Persona Workflow

This corresponds to the searcher acquisition workflow from earlier in the chapter is shown in Figure 4.4.

Thinking through the business goals for the content and creating an outline like the one in Figure 4.4 can help ensure every investment we make supports those goals and provides a concrete road map for building content.

The final page is obvious at first glance to contain the content that the searcher is looking for, as it includes a heading with Jud Pyle's name,

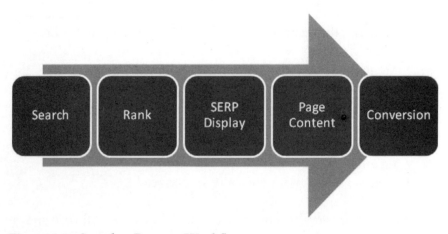

Figure 4.4   Searcher Persona Workflow

Figure 4.5   Clear Page Purpose

a large photo of him, and a biography. This helps ensure searchers don't abandon the page on first glance and keeps them engaged (see Figure 4.5).

To compel engagement, the page includes a prominent link to the RSS feed of Pyle's articles, as well as links to his video channels. Every page of the site has a clear sign up path (see Figures 4.6 and 4.7).

Once these pages are in place, you can use multivariate testing and other data to improve conversions.

Jud broadcasts the "Sidewinder" report from the floors of the Chicago Mercantile Exchange and the Chicago Board Options Exchange, co-hosts "Mad About Options" and is a regular contributor to "Options Physics." He regularly appears on CNBC, CNN, and Bloomberg.

Figure 4.6   Clear Calls to Action: Watch Videos

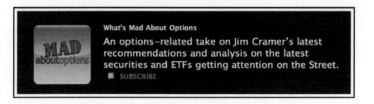

Figure 4.7 Clear Call to Action: Subscribe

Harnessing the Long Tail

One benefit of categorizing queries is that it helps you harness the long tail of search. The concept of the "long tail" was popularized by Chris Anderson's book by the same name.[3] The idea as it applies to search acquisition is that up to 80 percent of visitors might come from low-volume queries. For instance, in the case of O'Reilly, the site may get 100 visitors a day from the query [oreilly], and only two visitors a day from the query [conference about JavaScript for e-commerce Web sites]. However, the site may also get two visitors a day from [JavaScript conference for implementing product lists on the Web] and three visitors a day from [how to use JavaScript to build product pages]. In aggregate, the site may get 1,000 visits a day from conference-related queries, 1,500 visits a day from JavaScript-related queries, and 1,200 visits a day from e-commerce-related queries. So whereas individually, the two visits may seem insignificant, in aggregate, the visits from the low-volume query categories far outweigh the traffic from the highest-volume individual search.

While the resource investment for monitoring each individual query and providing content for it isn't reasonable, monitoring and building content for categories of queries is a manageable and worthwhile investment.

The Hotel without a Sign: Branded Search and the Importance of Title Tags

I stayed in a small town in Ireland recently and some friends and I drove through the main street, looking for a hotel we had decided to check out. (The town was too small for individual addresses. Instead, every business simply listed its name and the name of the town.) At one end of the village, we saw a large sign with a huge arrow pointing toward the direction of the hotel.

Aha. We had come to the beginning of the search funnel. We had a need (to get hotel rooms) and we knew the answer to that need (the specific hotel). That huge arrow was the beginning of our search.

But that's where things started to go off course. We drove down a small windy road with several forks, but no more signs for the hotel. We pressed ahead towards the water, thinking surely the hotel would be in that direction. The road ended at a parking lot and a large building that appeared abandoned. It vaguely resembled a hotel. The only sign was a small one over the door that read "hotel entrance." (See Figure 4.8.)

Was this in fact the hotel we were looking for? Whether it was or not, it was going to be our hotel for the night. Even though we were on a branded search (a search for a particular brand), the path wasn't clear. Had we seen another hotel on the way, we likely would have just stopped there, since we didn't have much confidence that we were going the right way. And we were resigned to staying at this hotel whether it was the right one or not. But apparently the hotel assumed everyone would just know where and who they were.

Can your site be found for searches for your brand? In a recent study, 55 percent of business to business buyers said that they would navigate to a site they already knew through search. You can see this trend in the top search terms. Nearly all are branded (see Figure 4.9).[4]

Enquiro Research has found that if a brand the searcher hadn't previously considered shows up in results, it is added to a consideration set 40 percent of the time.[5] And a brand not listed may be dropped from a consideration set. So, appearing in results is important even if the searcher doesn't click. In fact, Enquiro Research found a 16 percent lift in brand awareness when the brand appeared in both the top organic and top paid position (versus appearing in neither). When searchers were asked if they remembered seeing brands in the search results, fewer than 30 percent did if the brand was only in a paid search ad, but nearly 60 percent did when the brand appeared on top of both paid and organic. The study also found that appearance in the organic results only versus the paid results only causes more brand lift.

Figure 4.8   Is This the Hotel We Were Looking For?

Top 5 Paid and Organic Search Terms among All U.S. Websites				
Rank	Paid Terms	Clicks	Organic Terms	Clicks
1	ebay	0.12%	myspace	0.78%
2	ebay.com	0.02%	craigslist	0.42%
3	home depot	0.02%	myspace.com	0.29%
4	map quest	0.01%	youtube	0.26%
5	people search	0.01%	ebay	0.23%
Note - data is based on the percentage of paid and organic clicks generated by all search terms within all industry Categories for a four-week period ending Aug. 30, 2008 based off of the Hitwise sample of U.S. Internet users.				
Source: Hitwise				

Figure 4.9   Top 5 Search Terms

Source: Hitwise.com

And the positive brand perception doesn't stop at just recall. A 2006 iProspect and Jupiter Research study found that 36 percent of those surveyed felt that . . .

> . . . *seeing a company listed among the top results on a search engine makes me think that the company is a top one within its field.* . . .

Organic search should have a clear place in your brand awareness strategy. Visibility for your brand name, domain name, and primary tagline in organic searches should be a key requirement for any Web site initiative or advertising campaign. A quick search for [just do it] on the major search engines illustrates how this can easily go wrong even for large brands with a longstanding tagline (see Figure 4.10).[6]

Figure 4.10   Google Search Results: [Just Do It]

Source: Google Search Results

Review the result of the top ten organic search results for your brand. If negative items exist, can you add positive content to the Web (such as through social media, video and images, blog posts, interviews or articles on other sites, conference appearances, or media mentions) that could have the opportunity of outranking that negative content? Google calls this "proactively publishing information."[7]

Ensure any project that you do with an outside agency has organic search visibility as a project goal.

Track customer acquisition from branded organic search separately from other types of organic search and, if possible, track how the volume is influenced by other branding initiatives (such as display advertising).

You've Been Warned. Search: 2012

Sony Pictures built a marketing campaign around the movie *2012* that centered on search. Billboards cropped up sporting the cryptic message: "You've been warned. Search: 2012." The Search: 2012 tagline also was incorporated into other campaign elements, such as the movie trailer (see Figure 4.11).

At least in some cases, the campaign worked. A screenshot of the search results for [2012] on Flickr includes the description, "Spotted a

Figure 4.11   2012 the Movie Search Campaign

Figure 4.12 Google Search Results: [2012]

Source: Google Search Results

billboard off the 405 South in Gardena hyping the movie with this head-line above [search: 2012]. So of course I had to see what the fuss was all about (see Figure 4.12)."[8]

Google Insights for Search confirms that the campaigns have trig-gered search interest (see Figure 4.13).

Sony Pictures could further use Google Insights for Search to see how well the campaign is doing at a regional level by comparing search volume across cities to the billboard, television advertising, and other investments regionally (see Figure 4.14).

Unlike Hyundai, which, as we saw earlier, didn't appear in organic search results at all for the tagline they were promoting, the 2012 movie

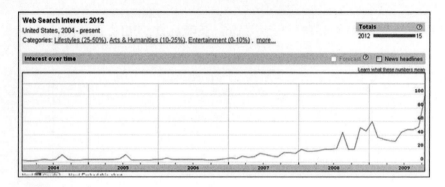

Figure 4.13 [2012] Search Trends

Source: Google Insights for Search

site appears number one on Google. Sony Pictures clearly is more focused on understanding how to be visible in organic search. However, including only the search term and not a Web site address in marketing material seems like a risky advertising strategy. Organic search results positions can't be guaranteed and are always fluctuating. And Sony Pictures has added to the risk by creating an all-Flash site, which as we'll learn in Chapter 7, can be problematic. Google does a much better job at indexing Flash than Microsoft Bing and Yahoo!, which could be contributing to the fact that the movie site does not rank number one on either of those search engines. Sony Pictures has further created search issues by maintaining several identical sites. Google and Yahoo! list who willsurvive2012.com (which, from a branding perspective, is likely the

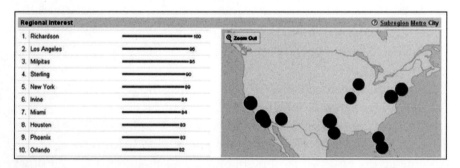

Figure 4.14 [2012] Regional Search Trends

Source: Google Insights for Search

site Sony Pictures is looking to promote). Microsoft, however, lists sony-pictures.com/movies/2012, which is simply a duplicate site. Why is this such a problem? Beyond the branding confusion, promoting two identical sites means that the links from other sites will be split between both of them (and in fact, as of this writing, both sites had approximately the same number of links). As a result, www.whowillsurvive2012.com has half the link value it otherwise would, and the site may never achieve the rankings it otherwise would. (See Chapter 5 for more information on how external links impact rankings.)

Sony Pictures has additional obstacles since it has chosen to promote a search term that is already well-covered online. The movie is about a real theory, which is the potential end of the world in 2012 as evidenced by the end of the Mayan calendar. Numerous Web sites exist about this theory. Sony Pictures risks having those who search based on seeing billboards clicking to survive2012.com or december212012.com and never realizing that the billboard was meant to promote a movie.

Fortunately for Sony Pictures, both Microsoft and Yahoo! have blended search elements that use data feeds to provide movie-related information at the top of any search page that appears to be for a movie.

Should advertising campaigns integrate organic search at all? Absolutely. Throughout this book, we've discussed how potential customers often turn to search first, so integrating it from the beginning meets your customers where they are. Keep the following in mind when incorporating organic search into an advertising campaign:

- Ensure someone on the team (whether that person is in-house or with the ad agency you're working with) fully understands the complexities of organic search, including content development, technical Web infrastructure, and external links.
- Assess the competitive landscape. If possible, drive search interest in a tagline that's not already well-covered by unrelated sites.
- Unless it negatively impacts the campaign, include a Web site address and not simply a search term.
- When creating a plan for technical implementation, involve the organic search expert at every stage of the process and ensure you are accounting for all likely queries, including company name, product name, tagline, and Web site address.

- Have your organic search expert help design solutions for common issues, including:

  → Micro sites that don't launch until the campaign starts, and, therefore, aren't available for search engine indexing in time for the initial searches.

  → All-Flash sites that don't provide unique URLs and textual content for the search engines to index.

  → Duplicate content that can slow down indexing and dilute link value (and subsequently, ranking).

  → Sites that redirect, preventing the promoted Web site address from ever being indexed.

Now that we've identified whom to target through organic search and how to target them, let's learn a little more about how search engines work and how to build Web sites that searchers can easily find.

Chapter 4 Checklist 1: Building Searcher Personas

❏ Refer to the business and Web site goals identified in Chapter 2.

❏ Gather the relevant keywords gathered in Chapter 2.

❏ Cluster keywords into categories based on topic and searcher intent.

❏ For each category, answer:

  ❏ What are these searchers trying to accomplish?

  ❏ What will help them accomplish this?

  ❏ What will compel them to conversion?

❏ For each category, identify the Web page that satisfies the audience need.

❏ How does that Web page display in search results (what is the title and description that will appear)?

❏ Does this page provide context about what the site is about?

❏ What on the page compels the visitor to conversion?

❏ What is the call to action?

Chapter 4 Checklist 2: Evaluating Existing Web Pages for Strategy Alignment

❏ What are you trying to accomplish with this page?
❏ What audience are you trying to attract?
❏ What is that audience searching for?
❏ Will this page best satisfy that search?
❏ Does this page provide context about what the site is about?
❏ What on the page compels the visitor to conversion?
❏ What is the call to action?

CHAPTER

How Search Engines Work

We've seen how searchers behave and how they interact with search re-sults. We've decided what queries we want our sites to be found for. How do search engines compile these lists?

The Evolution of Search Engines

In the emerging days of the Web, directories were built to help users navigate to various Web sites. Generally, these directories were created by hand—people categorized Web sites so users could browse to what they wanted. As the Web got larger, this effort became more difficult. "Web spiders" were created that "crawled" Web sites. Web spiders, also known as robots, are computer programs that follow links from known Web sites to other Web sites. These robots access those pages, download the contents of those pages (into a storage mechanism generi-cally referred to as an "index"), and add the links found on those pages to their list for later crawling.

While Web crawlers enabled the early search engines to have a larger list of sites than the manual method of collecting sites, they couldn't perform the other manual tasks of figuring out what the pages were about and ranking them in order of which ones were best. These search engines started working on computer programs that would help them do these things as well. For instance, computer programs could catalog all the words on a page to help figure out what those pages were about.

The Introduction of PageRank

Google's "PageRank" algorithm in 1998 was a big step forward in automatically cataloging and ranking Web sites.[1] This algorithm used data from the links on the Web to determine what pages were about and which pages were more popular and useful. Links were like votes for a site and the text from those links was used for cataloging them.

For instance, consider two Web pages. One is at the address www .myusedcars.com, and the other is at the address www.yourusedcars .com. Both contain text about cars and have the title "Used Cars." Five Web sites link to www.myusedcars.com. Three use the text "site about used cars" and two use the text "lots of used Fords" in the links. Ten sites link to www.yourusedcars.com. Five use the text "site about used cars" and the other five use the text "lots of used Hondas" in the links (see Figure 5.1).

Google's PageRank algorithm would use the information from the links to determine that both sites were about used cars. But when someone searched for "used cars," Google would show www.yourusedcars .com first because it had twice as many links to it (10 versus 5). In addition, when someone searched for "used Fords," Google would show www.yourusedcars.com, and, when someone searched for "used Hondas," Google would show www.yourusedcars.com.

While Google patented the specific PageRank algorithm, this general method of categorizing sites became the standard for search engines and the basis of how search engine technology has evolved.

While people still refer to "PageRank" as a major factor in ranking well in search engines, this reference is now simply shorthand for the hundreds of signals that search engines use to compile a list of the most relevant results possible for a query. We'll take a closer look at some of these signals throughout this chapter.

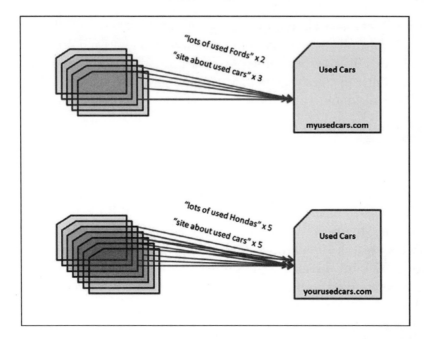

Figure 5.1 Anchor Text and Links Help Search Engines Understand Pages

The Current State of Search Engines

As the Web has evolved, a vast number of search engines have launched. They generally fall into one of the following categories:

- **Human-edited directories**—These are either constructed entirely by hand (as Yahoo! was originally) or constructed via a Web crawl or site owner submission and categorized and ranked by hand. Examples include the Open Directory Project (dmoz .org), About.com, and, more recently, Mahalo.com.
- **Automated search engines**—These are built algorithmically via Web crawlers and cataloged and ranked algorithmically as well. Since these types of search engines (such as Google) are the kind used by most searchers today, performing well in these is what this book focuses on.

- **Meta search engines (aggregators)**—These search engines generally use results from other search engines and present them in a different way either by presenting the results from multiple other engines together (such as dogpile.com) or with a different visual look.

How Search Engines Work

The major search engines that account for most market share today are the automated type: Google, Yahoo!, and Microsoft Bing[2] (although Yahoo! and Microsoft have reached an agreement in which Yahoo! will replace its search engine with Bing, although this hasn't happened as of late 2009[3]). All three, as well as other smaller search engines that exist and operate their own technology, have similar overall infrastructure as follows:

- Web crawlers (also known as "spiders" or "robots") that crawl the Web. These crawlers follow links to discover the pages on the Web.
- Extraction processes that gather information from those pages (such as textual content, metadata, and links).
- Index storage that stores the content from Web pages. Content is generally stored using word-based keys, similar to the index in a book. When you look up a word in the index of a book, you learn the page number that word is on. Similarly, with a search engine index, the search engine can look up a word that someone is searching for and find out all the Web pages associated with that word.
- Results scoring that determines what pages are the most relevant for each search. When someone does a search (called a "query") and the search engine checks the index for all the Web pages associated with that search, the search engine needs a way to rank those Web pages in an order that is useful for the searcher. Search engines use a number of factors in scoring and these factors are adjusted all of the time based on new algorithms, tests, and other criteria. Search engines keep the details of these scoring factors

secret. Once the search engine compiles and ranks the pages that are relevant for the query, it displays them in a list called "organic results." The ranking process happens at the time of the query.

The Difference between Organic and Paid Results

Search engines primarily make money via advertising called "paid search ads." These ads are also called pay per click (PPC) ads, because advertisers generally pay a certain amount each time a searcher clicks on them. For instance, Google's advertising program is called AdWords. The way the system works is that when someone does a search, the search engine shows two lists of results: organic and paid (see Figure 5.2).

The organic results are based on the crawling, indexing, and results scoring infrastructure, and search engines strive to have the most comprehensive, relevant results they can to provide an optimal user experience. Most search engines (such as Google) don't accept payment for placement in the organic results, and make no guarantees about whether

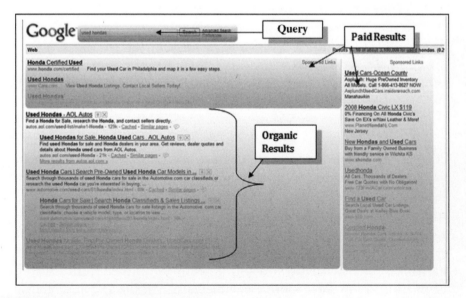

Figure 5.2   Search Results Page

a site is indexed and where that site will rank. The paid search ads appear beside the organic results, and while search engines also attempt to show relevant, useful results in their ads, companies pay for them. Paid search ads are the primary source of income for search engines.

How Search Engines Rank Results

As Google noted in mid-2009:

> *"Ranking is hard, much harder than most people realize. One reason for this is that languages are inherently ambiguous, and documents do not follow any set of rules. There are really no standards for how to convey information, so we need to be able to understand all Web pages, written by anyone, for any reason. And that's just half of the problem. We also need to understand the queries people pose, which are on average fewer than three words, and map them to our understanding of all documents. Not to mention that different people have different needs. And we have to do all of that in a few milliseconds . . . By some estimates, more than one thousand pro-grammer/scientist years have gone directly into their [search engines'] development, and the rate of innovation has not slowed down."*
>
> *"The life span of a Google query normally lasts less than half a second, yet involves a number of different steps that must be completed before results can be delivered to a person seeking information."*[4]

Search engines use a number of factors to determine how to rank content. At a high level, search engines associate each set of content with a set of keywords they determine that content is about. When a searcher performs a query, the search engine retrieves all of the pages that are associated with that query, orders them according to rele-vance and usefulness (based on things like the number of relevant external links pointing to those pages, the anchor text of those exter-nal links, and calculations about intent—for instance, the search engine will try to show more e-commerce sites if the searcher intends to purchase something), and then ensures the resulting set of pages has sufficient diversity (doesn't include duplicates or doesn't consist of only sites of a single type).

How Search Engines Are Using Data About Searcher Intent

Over time, as search engines have gotten more confident about understanding intent, they've become more aggressive about displaying what they think the searchers want. Overall, this is a good thing because they're providing what searchers are looking for even more quickly, without requiring searchers to make extra choices. Most searchers aren't power users and just want to type the words into a search box and get back the results they're looking for with as little work as possible (remember bounded rationality?).

Search Engine Suggestions and Prompts

As noted earlier in Query Refinements on page 66, search engines incorporate many methods for integrating browser navigation into the search experience to enable searchers to drill into what they're really searching for. These search prompts are typically based on past searcher behavior. For instance, Google lists related searches, Bing provides search categories, and Yahoo! includes an "explore related topics" pane.

Paying attention to what the search engines suggest for topics important to your business can both give you insight into what your potential customers are really looking for and help you understand how your company should be represented in search results.

Personalization

Search engines customize results based on individual searcher behavior. They continue to ramp up their efforts over time to understand not only searcher intent in aggregate, but also intent for specific searchers.

Search engines need to provide relevant results to searchers (so that they'll keep coming back to that search engine and be an audience for its advertising); and because searchers provide few clues about what they're really looking for, we've seen that search engines use aggregate knowledge to discern meaning. But searchers are individuals, not the sum of their aggregated searches, so extrapolating the intent of one search based on the actions of all the searches that came before can rarely provide results as relevant as those tailored to the individual searcher.

Over the years, search engines have tried various customization options to enable searchers to take an active role in improving their results—everything from sliders to adjust ranking factors, filtering specific types of files, date ranges, and type of content.

But even though all of these could indeed improve results, for the most part, searchers have overwhelmingly ignored them. One reason for this goes back, again, to the idea of "bounded rationality."

Usability expert Jakob Nielson describes this tendency as follows:

"The basic information foraging theory, which is, I think, the one theory that basically explains why the Web is the way it is, says that people want to expend minimal effort to gain their benefits. And this is an evolutionary point that has come about because the people, or the creatures who don't exert themselves, are the ones most likely to survive when there are bad times or a crisis of some kind. So people are inherently lazy and don't want to exert themselves. Picking from a set of choices is one of the least effortful interaction styles which is why this point and click interaction in general seems to work very well . . . [w]hereas tweaking sliders, operating pull down menus and all that stuff—that is just more work."[5]

So the search engines have begun inferring customizations for searchers, rather than requiring them to explicitly set them. Search engines use a number of methods for personalizing search results. For instance, the engines may take into account what sites you've clicked on before and the ones you never click on, no matter how highly they're ranked. Google also takes the previous search into account. If you search for [Hawaii vacations] and then search for [flights], Google may show you flight information for Hawaii, even though the word "Hawaii" wasn't in the second search. If you have the Google Toolbar installed, Google will even track the sites you visit independently of those you reached from Google and will use those to shape your search results.[6]

And while the current influence of personalization at Google is subtle, these efforts continue to advance. Google's Marissa Mayer noted:

> *"The actual implementation of personalized search is that as many as two pages of content, that are personalized to you, could be lifted onto the first page and I believe they never displace the first result, because that's a level of relevance that we feel comfortable with. So right now, at least eight of the results on your first page will be generic, vanilla Google results for that query and only up to two of them will be results from the personalized algorithm. I think the other thing to remember is, even when personalization happens and lifts those two results onto the page, for most users it happens one out of every five times.*
>
> *I think that overall, we really feel that personalized search is something that holds a lot of promise, and we're not exactly sure of the signals that will yield the best results. We know that search history, your clicks and your searches together provide a really rich set of signals, but it's possible that some of the other data that Google gathers could also be useful. It's a matter of understanding how."[7]*

Frequent Google spokesperson Matt Cutts has also intimated that personalization is likely to increase:

> *"The idea of a monolithic set of search results for a generic term will probably start to fade away, and you already see people expect that if I do a search and somebody else does the search, they can get slightly different answers. I expect that over time people will expect that more and more."[8]*

In December 2009, Google expanded how they personalize results, causing search expert Danny Sullivan to comment that "The days of 'normal' search results that everyone sees are now over. Personalized results are the 'new normal,' and the change is going to shift the search world and society in general in unpredictable ways."[9] With this change, Google is now personalizing everyone's results, not just the ones of those searchers who are logged in. If the searcher isn't logged in, Google uses the search history from that computer to personalize results. Why is this such a radical shift in the search world? Because there's no longer a base set of results. Now, more than ever, rankings reports don't have much meaning.

Google says they won't skew things so much that searching narrows our view of the online world. Google product manager Johanna Wright explained, "We want diversity of results. This is something we talk about a lot internally and believe in. We want there to be a variety of sources and opinions in the Google results. We want them in personalized search to be skewed to the user, but we don't want that to mean the rest of the web is unavailable to them."

Anatomy of a Search Engine Result

On page 75, we looked at how the search results are displayed and how important it is to ensure your site has a compelling listing. Let's look a little more closely.

A Search Engine Results Page (SERP) typically contains 10 results for a query. Each search result contains the following results (see Figure 5.3).

1. **Title:** This is generally the same as the title of the page. (See page 164 for more details on influencing this.)
2. **Snippet:** This is the description beneath the title. This is your main opportunity to provide a marketing message to searchers

Figure 5.3 A Typical Search Result

Source: Google Search Results

to entice them to click through to your site. (See page 165 for more details on influencing this.)
3. **URL:** The URL of the page. Any keywords from the query are bolded.

Search results can include a number of other components as well, such as (see Figure 5.4):

- Navigational links to sections within the site.
- The date the page was published.
- Links to forum content.
- Rating and review information.

The Evolution of Organic Search Results: Beyond Web Pages

Originally, search engines indexed text on Web pages and matched text-based searches to that content. As the Web evolved, search engines began looking at ways to catalog the new types of content on Web pages, such as video and images. They created "vertical" indices that enabled searchers to look specifically for images, for instance. However, search engines found that few searchers noticed these vertical indices and that most searchers looked for everything from the main search page.

In 2007, Google introduced "universal search," a new way of compiling results that blended content from all of their indices, including textual Web content, images, videos, news, and product listings.[10] The other major search engines soon implemented their own versions of "blended search" and today, it's common to see all of these things appearing together in search results (see Figure 5.5).

Official **Monopoly Rules** Page
Jump to **BUYING PROPERTY**: Whenever you land on an unowned **property** you may **buy** that **property** from the Bank at its printed price. ...
OBJECT - EQUIPMENT - PREPARATION - BANKER
richard_wilding.tripod.com/monorules.htm - Cached - Similar

Figure 5.4   Links within a Search Result
Source: Google Search Results

Figure 5.5   Google Multimedia Search Results
Source: Google Search Results

This blending provides opportunity for site owners. Now, in addition to listing your textual content, you can showcase your multimedia content as well.

When searchers see blended results, they view the page in a slightly different way than when the results are text only. Look at this eye tracking heat map from Enquiro (see Figure 5.6).

Most searchers looked at the image and, in fact, more than looked to the results below the image (d) than to those above it (b).

The appearance of non-textual content in the search results continues to rise. Marissa Mayer, VP of Search Products and Experience for Google, noted:

"I think there's a ton of challenges, because in my view, search is in its infancy, and we're just getting started. I think the most pressing, immediate need as far as the search interface is to break the

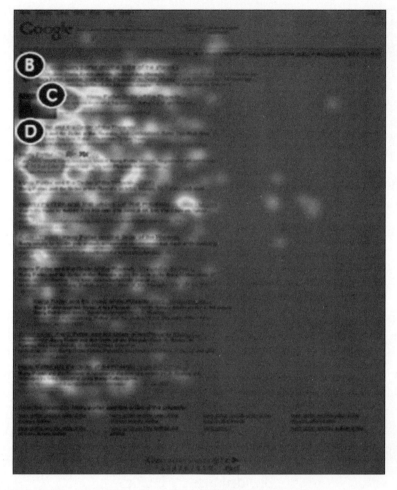

Figure 5.6   Eye Tracking Heat Map: Multimedia Results
Source: Enquiro

paradigm of the expectation of "You give us a keyword, and we give you 10 URLs.

We need to look at results pages that aren't just 10 standard URLs that are laid out in a very linear format. Sometimes the best answer is a video, sometimes the best answer will be a photo, and sometimes the best answer will be a set of extracted facts. If I type in general demographic statistics about China, it'd be great if

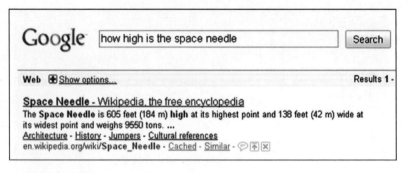

Figure 5.7   Google Answers Questions In Search Results
Source: google.com

I got a set of facts that had been parsed off of and even aggregated and cross-validated across a result set."[11]

And in fact, Google has begun providing more answers in their search results, in a way very similar to what Marissa Mayer described. In January 2010, Google began using its Google Squared service[12] to extract facts from web pages and display them in the search results.[13] For instance, with the query [how high is the space needle], Google no longer simply lists the pages that might contain this information, but surfaces the answer in the search results in Figure 5.7.

The next section of this chapter discusses content beyond Web pages that has become standard in search results.

Blended Search: Images

One common type of blended result is images. To see the value of blended image search results in action, let's return to my trip to Bologna. I had heard that I should visit the church of San Luca, but I knew nothing about it. So, I went over to Google and typed in [San Luca Bologna], hoping to find a description and perhaps a map. But Google (likely based on the clicks of millions who had come before me) knew my intent even better than I did, and showed me not only descriptive details and a map, but also images (see Figure 5.8).

Even though I didn't know I was looking for them, the images caught my attention first (even though I had been specifically thinking

I was looking for a map!). I clicked on the image at the far right and came across a *Telegraph* article about Bologna, which in turn led me to some great information about local hotels, restaurants, and shops (see Figure 5.9).

And so, blended search and PR have joined together with search to bring more visitors to the businesses of Italy. (See page 189 for

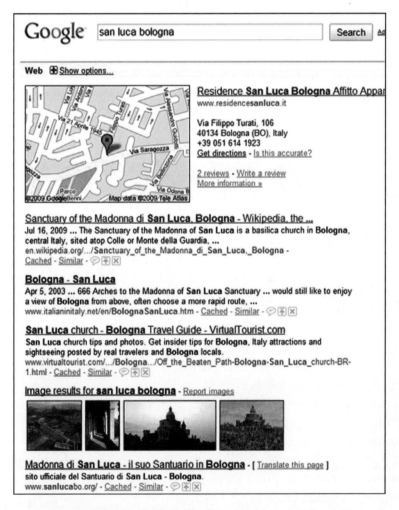

Figure 5.8   Google Image Search Results: [San Luca Bologna]

Source: Google Search Results

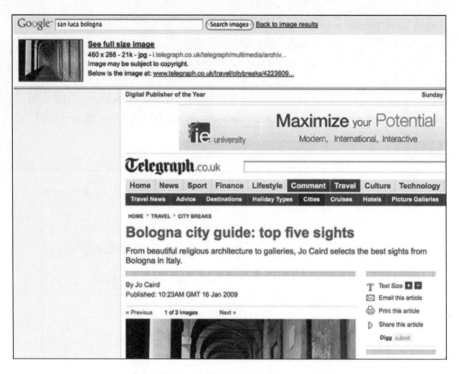

Figure 5.9   Acquisition from Google Image Search Results
Source: Google Image Search

more information on how PR can work together with search for better visibility.)

From there, I clicked "Back to image results" and then to another image found on virtualtourist.com (see Figure 5.10).

I continued to explore "off the beaten path" tips, and just like that, Virtual Tourist gained a user.

Of course, tourism isn't the only industry that can gain search acquisition from images. One of the bigger industries image searches can lead customers to is e-commerce.

Let's say, for instance, that I'm looking for blue and white plates. The easiest way to research them may be to simply do a search, which gives me the results in Figure 5.11.

I can start my shopping on NexTag or Amazon, but if I'm not sure yet exactly *which* blue and white plates I want to buy, the image results

Figure 5.10   Google Images Search Results for Long Term Acquisition
Source: Google Image Search

seem like a great place to start. If I dive into the full list of images, I can not only see all of the different choices (critical for a purchase such as this one), but I can also choose between auctions, set replacements, and new retail.

As you might imagine, the search conversion workflow becomes critical here. If the site design doesn't take into account a visitor from an

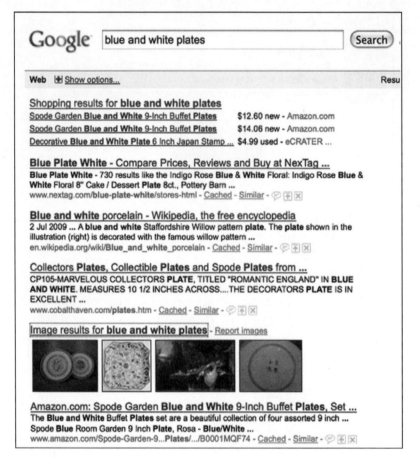

Figure 5.11   Google Image Search Results: [blue and white plates]
Source: Google Search Results

image search who may come directly to the page that contains the image, vital information about the site, its navigation, and how to order may not be present, and many visitors may be unsure how to proceed and might go back to the search results.

The Drayton Hall site provides a great experience for a visitor coming from an image search. The site, its value proposition, the overall navigation, and the item price and path to purchase are readily apparent (see Figure 5.12).

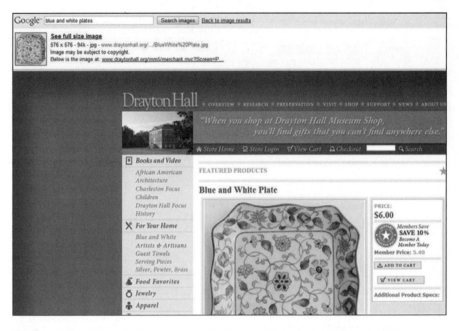

Figure 5.12   Google Image Search Results E-commerce Acquisition

Source: Google Image Search

On the other hand, the Yoko Webster page provides no information at all (see Figure 5.13).

In addition to blended search opportunities for images, searchers conduct more than a billion image-specific searches a month, indicating that image optimization definitely shouldn't be overlooked.[14]

How can you best take advantage of this? Make sure your site includes images where they're useful, particularly if you're selling products. And ensure your Web development team implements images in a search-friendly way. (Page 162 talks a bit more about image optimization.)

Blended Search: Video

Video provides another big opportunity for search acquisition. Not only do videos often appear in blended search results, but YouTube is now

Figure 5.13   Each Page Should Provide a Next Step

Source: Google Image Search

the second largest search engine (after Google). You can now submit product videos to Google Product Search[15] as well, so clearly video opportunity continues to increase. And views of online video increased 41 percent from August, 2008, to August, 2009,[16] so potential customer behavior continues to evolve from primarily consuming text online to being comfortable consuming video as well. We conduct more than 2.6 billion searches a month on video search engines.[17] Eighty-five percent of online Americans view videos online each month, for a total of 26 billion video views.[18]

People love videos. Tutorials, for instance, provide a great opportunity for video as a complement to textual instructions.

Assess your site for video opportunities, create a YouTube channel for your videos, and make sure that as with web pages, you use descriptive text that uses the language of your target audience (see Figure 5.14).

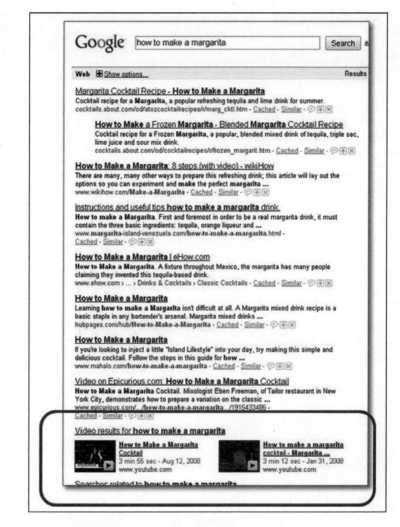

Figure 5.14   Video Results in Google Search

Source: google.com

How Do Universal Results Impact Searcher Behavior?

Enquiro's eye tracking studies found that when an image or video is present in the top half of the search results, the searcher seems to start the page scan there, rather than the top left.[19] (See Figure 5.15.)

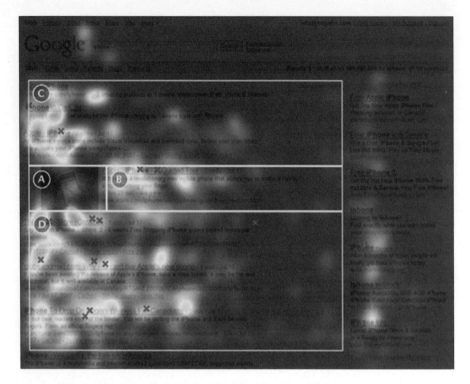

Figure 5.15   Eye Tracking Heat Map: Video Search Results
Source: Enquiro Research

In a text-only set of results, searchers begin in the top left corner, scan right, and then down, and they tend to chunk the page into result sets of 3–4 results and evaluate those one by one. If searchers don't find the answer in the first chunk, they move on to the next one.

In results that contain multimedia such as video and images, searchers started with the multimedia result as the first chunk and then scanned above it for the second chunk and below it for the third chunk (see Figure 5.16).

Similarly, when a Local Onebox is on the page, searchers tend to evaluate the local listings as a separate chunk.

Clearly, optimizing for images and video is useful not only because it provides additional ranking opportunities, but also because it enables you to stand out to searchers over the competition.

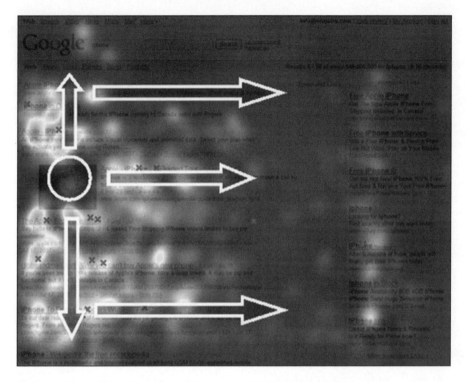

Figure 5.16   How Searchers Interact with Multimedia Results
Source: Enquiro Research

Internationalization

A notable influence on personalized results is regional location. Location-tailored results can be a substantial part of the relevance calculation. At a basic level, all results are personalized based on location. A searcher in the United States will get more results from U.S./English-language Web sites, whereas a searcher in Italy will get more results from Italian Web sites written in Italian. In addition, certain queries have additional location-based relevance factors. For instance, someone searching for [pizza] in Seattle is likely to see Seattle-based restaurant results and someone searching for [pizza] in Boston will likely see Boston-based restaurant results.

Regional relevance factors are particularly important to businesses that are local in nature (such as pizza restaurants) and those that serve particular countries (British Telecom would like its site to be surfaced to British searches; HP would like its Spanish site to be served to Spanish searchers). These factors get trickier as the intent becomes more complicated. What about U.S. searchers who are looking for vacation accommodations in Croatia? Or a French speaker on vacation in Italy who is looking for information about trains in Poland? And how should businesses target the European Union? Or how should a business target researchers in Mexico, rather than in Spain, with Spanish content?

Internationalization for search acquisition is beyond the scope of this book, but check marketingintheageofgoogle.com for resources.

Getting Technical: How It All Comes Together

Now, for the technical part. But don't worry! I'm not asking you to go make changes to the servers yourself! Chapter 7 contains more details about working with web developers and ensuring that they're using search-friendly best practices.

Crawling

Before a search engine can evaluate the content on your site to determine if it's relevant for a searcher's query, the engine has to know the page exists and extract that content from the site for analysis.

1. **Discovering the pages:** Search engines find out about pages on the Web generally by following links from other sites on the Web and by following a site's internal links. The most important thing to remember about the discovery process is that you should build a great site that makes others want to link to it and that you should have a comprehensive site navigation structure. Of course, you'd want both of these things on your site even if search engines didn't exist.
2. **Crawling the pages:** Once a search engine such as Google learns about pages on the Web, it uses a "bot" to crawl those

pages. Your goal is likely to have your entire site crawled, which can be hindered by crawling inefficiencies and by infrastructure issues that make URLs inaccessible to the bots.

3. **Extracting content:** Once a crawler has accessed a page, it has to be able to extract the content from that page and store it. As with crawling, a number of obstacles may keep a search engine from extracting content from your pages. Common issues include all Flash sites, pages full of multimedia such as videos and images with no textual markup, and sites built on technologies such as AJAX that search engines can have trouble parsing. A good rule of thumb is that if you develop the site using progressive enhancement techniques[20] that make it accessible for visitors with disabilities[21] (who are using devices such as screen readers to access your site) and on mobile devices, search engines can generally access the content as well.

Indexing

Once the crawler has accessed the pages and extracted the content, the search engines make a decision about whether to store that content. They'll generally not store pages if they determine that those pages are mostly empty, are duplicates of pages they've already stored, or have little value (for instance, the pages may be an aggregation of content that exists elsewhere on the Web). One common cause of duplicate content is syndication. (See page 166 for more information.)

Ranking

Crawling and indexing issues tend to be technical in nature. It can be vital for Web developers to understand these parts of the process to ensure the site's technical infrastructure isn't blocking the search engine bots. Ranking, on the other hand, is primarily dependent on how relevant a page is for the given query. If you build searcher personas and incorporate search data into your product development processes, you are already taking the important steps toward ensuring your pages are as relevant as possible to the searchers you are targeting. As noted above, relevant, authoritative links also help search engines understand the value of your site's pages, and those come naturally with useful content and a successful marketing strategy.

According to leaked 2008 Google quality guidelines, utility (how helpful the page is for the searcher based on intent), "is the most important aspect of search engine quality."[22]

Once you start to think about personalization, differing results based on searcher location, and blended search results that may cause the searcher's attention to focus on a result other than the top-ranked site, you start to realize why ranking reports don't provide much actionable insight. (We'll look at that more closely in Chapter 8.)

CHAPTER

Implementing an Effective Search Strategy

In previous chapters, we learned how to use the intersection of search data and business needs to identify effective Web site content strategies, as well as a little about how search engines work. How can we bring this information together into our organizations so that our content strategies are effective for search?

At a high level, in order to effectively use organic search as an acquisition channel, companies should ensure their Web sites can:

- Be discovered by search engines so their pages can be added to the list the crawler uses to traverse the Web.
- Be accessible to the crawler (build the site architecture so that it doesn't introduce obstacles).
- Have extractable information (ensure content isn't inaccessible).
- Be relevant and useful to searchers.

Sounds easy, right? The good news is that the path to success is fairly straightforward. But as you might imagine, the devil is in the details. The practice of ensuring that sites implement all of these things in a way that searchers can find them is known as search engine optimization (SEO).

However, as we've seen, for a business to be effective online long term, it has to think of search as a key part of all aspects of its organization, and not as a separate activity. And the term "search engine optimization" is a bit of a misnomer because it implies that you're optimizing your site for search engines when in reality you're optimizing your site for your audience (who often are searchers) and ensuring your site is built to be successful in an online environment.

You may in fact need a point person to ensure that search acquisition best practices are being built out within your organization, particularly if your organization is in the early stages of building out that process.

This book isn't about how to tactically implement search engine optimization. A number of books, conferences, and sites exist about tactical SEO implementation.

If you are interested in the tactical details of SEO, check out Searchengineland.com (where I'm an editor), the Search Marketing Expo conferences,[1] and my site, janeandrobot.com, for technical techniques. More information is located on my resources page at marketingintheageofgoogle.com.

This book is about how to think strategically about search and how your business fits into a search-based culture. With that in mind, this chapter talks about what's required to implement search best practices within an organization and the following chapter talks about working with developers.

Would You Like to Exchange Links with My Site Buy-Cheap-Viagra-While-You-Play-Poker-Online-and-File-a-Mesothelioma-Class-Action-lawsuit.info?

The phrase "search engine optimization" tends to bring up bad memories of e-mails asking you to trade links and Web pages with repeated words but no real information and no place to click but on ads.

"Search engine optimization" implies optimizing a site for search engines, but understanding how search fits into your business isn't really about that at all. It's about operating your business effectively within the current landscape. If you have retail stores, you likely have a real estate specialist scouting out locations. If your product appeals to teenage girls ages 13–17, you'll want to do market research to find out what they like. As we've seen, search strategy is no different.

But still the term SEO is often more associated with buy-cheap-Viagra-while-you-play-poker-online-and-file-a-mesothelioma-class-action-lawsuit than it is with customer engagement, usability, product strategy, and more sales.

Consider this recent posting on a tech startup e-mail list (emphasis mine):

> *We are in dire need of a customer experience/consumer experience expert . . . Does anyone have any suggestions for partners/firms/consultants to reach out to in order to try to find adequate partners to assure that the consumer's needs and issues are addressed?* (**Not SEO experts**—*usability or consumer experience experts for e-commerce*).

And yet the description is exactly what good SEO should be: understanding and improving the customer experience.

On an entrepreneur forum, someone posted that 95 percent of SEO is useless. He went on to write:

> *Some of the tactics I've seen "SEO professionals" sell are:*
>
> 1. *Link farms—This goes into my pile of 95 percent of the SEO tactics that shouldn't be used.*
> 2. *Code all content within H1 tags.*
> 3. *Code all content within anchor tags.*
> 4. *Put title attributes on all content.*
> 5. *Make the content as verbose and wordy as possible.*
> 6. *Put your top 20 keywords in all image & file names.*
> 7. *Paying forum/blog . . . spammers.*

Yet, nothing he's listed there is an "SEO tactic." All of these items are spammer tricks (and not even ones that are generally used anymore).

What he's said is similar to saying that 95 percent of what painters do is a scam, and then listing as that 95 percent things like substituting cheaper paint and charging you for the expensive stuff, painting only one wall when you paid for all four, and spraying graffiti rather than painting the room.

Any legitimate painter would have good cause to protest that none of those things are painting tactics.

Let's take a look at just a few more viewpoints on SEO found from around the Web:

1. "Many of the so-called 'SEO professionals' are not much more than modern snake oil salesmen. They game and manipulate the system for their own intentions."[2]
2. "Everyone uses Google for search, and therefore online businesses need to be found on Google, which means you need to do Search Engine Optimization. SEO is the worst thing ever invented. It's destroying good Web application development."[3]
3. "I actually despise being labeled an SEO. Why? SEOs are like the 21st century car salesmen. Most are slimy and have no clue what they are talking about. They tell you [that] you just need to put spammy keywords in your title tag, keyword tag, and write a spammy as hell description metatag."[4]
4. "Search Engine Optimization is not a legitimate form of marketing. It should not be undertaken by people with brains or souls."[5]

The perception of the SEO profession may have hit one of its lowest moments in August 2009, when Fox News published a story entitled "Top Online Marketing Jobs to Leave You Friendless." The article states:

Job-hunting? Think about becoming an e-mail spammer . . . or a Web site spammer . . . or a search engine optimizer. Here's a great opportunity to become part of a team of Web-savvy professionals who clog the Internet with unwanted ads and sell users' personal information to the highest bidder. Not only are these jobs legal, they can be downright lucrative. Here are some of the top online marketing jobs that will make you money . . . and leave you alone and friendless.

Search Engine Optimizer

Ever wonder why "nonsense" Web sites sometimes turn up in your search results on Google or Yahoo!? That's because search engine optimizing scammers work full-time to create thousands of other Web sites that link to the spam site.[6]

Of course, that doesn't actually describe a search engine optimizer. It describes a Web spammer.

Beyond SEO

I don't know if the term "SEO" can be reclaimed. While the negative perception about SEO is inaccurate, it is the case that a subset of those who practice SEO tend to narrowly focus on rankings, rather than customer experience. This certainly isn't true of all who practice SEO, but it's hard to distinguish when we're using the same name to describe both types of practices. And, as mentioned earlier in this chapter, the term "search engine optimization" doesn't describe well the whole picture of integrating a search acquisition strategy into a more comprehensive business strategy.

Throughout this book, I've used "search acquisition strategy" to describe this effort, which includes:

- Using search data to build a comprehensive and effective product and content strategy.
- Understanding searcher behavior and building searcher personas that maximize customer satisfaction and conversions.
- Realizing the customer acquisition funnel begins with the search box.
- Integrating organic search with other marketing efforts.
- Ensuring the technical architecture of the site can be properly crawled and indexed by search engines so it can be visible to searchers.

When I look at organic search acquisition, I'm looking from a point of triangulation. I understand that searchers want the best result as quickly as possible. I understand that search engines want to understand the Web so they can deliver the most relevant results. And I understand that site owners want to market their content effectively to the right audience.

We've talked about using search data, building a comprehensive strategy, creating searcher personas, and engaging with customers. But what do your product marketers, content writers, and Web developers need to know about their roles in ensuring your search strategy is effective?

Web Architecture

- Web development teams should build Web sites in such a way that they can be easily crawled and indexed by search engines. (We talk about this in Chapter 7.)
- Upper management should provide the necessary support for making infrastructure search-engine friendly.
- Upper management should state requirements in terms of functional outcomes (an easy to navigate menu system) rather than implementation (a Flash menu).
- The content management system and content modification process should easily allow for non-technical staff to update important content sections of the site, such as the title, headings, and paragraphs.

Strategic Development

- Those doing market research, determining product features, building a product road map, or developing a company vision should understand the value of search data and how to effectively make use of it.
- All marketing goals should be shared and all marketing silos (such as offline advertising, online advertising, and e-mail marketing) should share data and understand how one channel impacts the rest.

Content Development

Content writers should understand keyword research, searcher behavior, and how to build searcher personas.

No one should build a page without knowing the answers to the questions:

- What is the goal of this page? What is the conversion event and call to action?
- Why would a visitor land on this page? What would he or she want to get from it?
- Why would that visitor then want to follow the call to action?

Advertising Initiatives

- Any offline campaigns should include an organic search component. What searches might this campaign drive and what is the searcher experience?
- Any ad agencies building Web content to support offline campaigns should have search-friendliness as a default requirement.

Becoming Too Focused on SEO

As already noted, this book is not about how to tactically implement SEO. This book is about how to think strategically about search and how your business fits into a search-based culture.

There is, however, one point of tactical SEO that is important to convey to your organization. If you read search blogs, attend search conferences, and otherwise follow the search industry, it's easy to get caught up in the particulars of the search engine algorithms. How many times should a particular word be repeated? How many links should any given page have? How many words should be on any given page? Chasing the answers to these questions can have vast opportunity cost and little gain. The search engine algorithms are in a constant state of flux. Experts are tweaking settings every day to see how they can make results a little more relevant. If you spend your time "optimizing" your site for these algorithmic particulars, you'll never have time to do anything else.

A much better strategy is to focus on what the search engines are trying to achieve with all of those algorithm tweaks—showing the most relevant results for a given query. Ensure your technical team gets the foundational infrastructure elements right (as described in Chapter 7) and ensure your marketing and product teams build the right features and content. This will not only get you ranking well, but will help you achieve what you're really after—which is not rankings, but customers.

Search Engine Guidelines and Penalties

The search engines have published guidelines.[7] Violate any of those guidelines and you risk having your site demoted in ranking or removed from the index. The spirit behind the search engine guidelines is that the search engines reserve the right to take action on any sites that intentionally try to manipulate their ranking algorithms—which makes sense, since core to the search engines is the relevance of their results. If sites are manipulating those results and making them less relevant and useful to searchers, the engines have methods of pinpointing that and adjusting for it.

The search engines (and Google in particular) have published a number of examples of what might constitute results manipulation. Generally, these are pretty straightforward and likely sound very similar to the spammy tactics the SEO naysayers incorrectly attribute to SEO. But the examples also serve as a check for those who aren't spammers who may have lost sight of what's really important about search acquisition in their focus on rankings.

Building Search into the Process of the Organization

By now, you know that a successful search acquisition strategy relies on weaving search best practices throughout the organization. This becomes difficult as business activities can be segmented from each other, departments may have political reasons for not collaborating with others, and some organizational processes simply aren't built for this type of cross-department collaboration.

The key is support from the top down. If upper management provides a central search goal that can be shared by all parts of the organization and provides the resources necessary for search integration, individual departments are motivated and empowered to embrace search best practices.

Below are some best practices to consider weaving into the organization.

Content Architecture

We've seen, at a high level, how search engines work and how searchers interact with results. Beyond what topics you choose to include on your site, which clearly have a significant impact on the audience you attract, what should you think about when building content?

- **Ensure the site has useful information architecture.** Do multiple pages have similar content? Will visitors be confused about which page to access to get the information they want? Consider this results listing for [small business intuit]. Having many pages about the same topic makes for confusing search results, an overwhelming user experience, and unnecessary maintenance overhead (see Figure 6.1).
- **Ensure the content uses the language of the customer.** Make sure anyone writing copy understands keyword research (Chapter 2) and uses it as part of the writing process. And make sure the organization has a process in place that keeps track of this research. Too often, I see companies spend significant time and energy researching customer language and crafting engaging messaging, only to have another department or outside agency later revise the content without realizing the work that had been done and removing all of those carefully researched words.

  One potential method for keeping track of the words customers use to search is to indicate the ones chosen for the page focus in the meta keywords tag[8] of the page. The contents of this tag aren't used by search engines for organic search, but can be

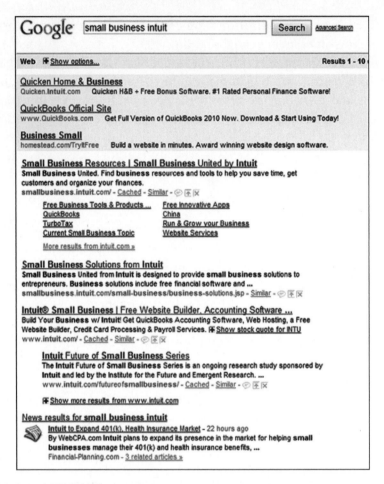

Figure 6.1 Google Search Results: [small business intuit]

Source: Google Search Results

helpful for internal communication. Depending on the content management system your organization uses and what internal processes you have in place, determine best practices for communicating these types of details on a page level.

- **Use standard HTML components on the page.** Once you've determined the key content for the page (for instance, "natural arthritis treatments"), ensure that content appears in the page's title, primary heading, and textual content. Remember that based

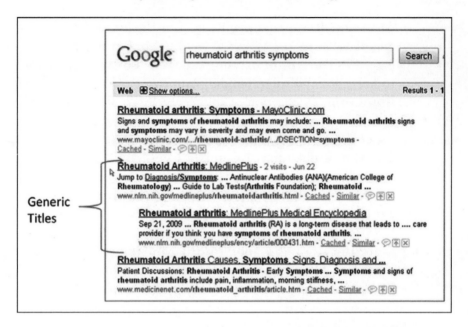

Figure 6.2   Google Search Results: [rheumatoid arthritis symptoms]

on how searchers skim search results pages, you should put the most important keywords in the far left of the title. And you should qualify phrases as fully as possible without being overwhelming ("Canon X54T Digital Camera with Zoom" rather than "X54T"). (See Figure 6.2.)

- **Remember that every page of the site is a potential entry page for visitors.** As we discussed in Chapter 4, every page should:
  - Clearly indicate the primary topic.
  - Help the visitor complete a task.
  - Provide orientation and contextual information about the site.
  - Motivate the visitor into the acquisition funnel with a compelling call to action. As we discussed, every page needs a clear call to action. Pages can suffer from no call to action (remember the PEAK6 personality pages) or too many calls to action. Without a clear call to action, all the work to get the page crawled, indexed, and ranked was for nothing.[9]

- **Answer visitor questions.** Remember the list of questions we generated using the Wordtracker Keyword questions tool on page 45? The type of phrasing searchers use can be important to keep in mind when building content, particularly for sites that provide a collection of answers or FAQs about their business. For instance, answers.oreilly.com provides information about the most commonly asked questions in technology. The company would attract far greater acquisition from search if it worded its headings as questions, much as people would search for them, rather than as answers. So, for instance, "How Do I Set Up a Relational Database with Rails" rather than "How to Set Up a Relational Database with Rails."
- **Ensure the site has a good internal linking structure.** This is vital for an easily crawlable site. At least one link should exist to every page (a good HTML site map helps provide this, as well as gives visitors a browsable architecture) and the links should use descriptive anchor text.[10]

It's important to think about what to link to from your home page. This is the page that most visitors will see, so it makes sense that you would want your most important pages to be linked to it. Search engines know this too, so they can use this link architecture as a signal of importance.

Sites can go overboard with this though. As soon as someone starts thinking about how to structure links solely in terms of how the search engines might interpret them and not in terms that make sense for visitors, the usability of the site declines and search engines (which are on to these tactics) can no longer use these signals to determine relevance.

Marketing, Advertising, and Public Relations

We know that organic search should be integrated into other marketing activities—everything from market research to Super Bowl commercials. What do the marketing, advertising, and public relations departments need to know about search?

- **Your customers are also searchers.** For any advertising campaign you undertake, ensure organic search is part of the planning process. What taglines and products are you promoting? What might your advertising efforts cause your audience to search for? Do you have pages on your Web site devoted to those things and can search engines access them?
- **Searchers are also your customers.** The people you are trying to attract through search are the same people you are trying to attract through e-mail campaigns, other online and offline advertising campaigns, press releases, and other channels. Share data and you may be amazed at how much more complete a picture you can get of your audience and how much better you will be able to provide them with a compelling, consistent experience.
- **Be wary of all Flash sites and micro sites.** We'll talk about this a bit more in Chapter 7, but advertising agencies sometimes build micro sites and Flash sites as part of a campaign. There's nothing inherently wrong with either tactic, but both require a bit of extra attention to ensure their content can be easily found by search engines. Make sure your ad agency knows that searchability is part of the project requirements.
- **Understand online reputation management.** When someone searches for your brand, what types of results appear? Ensuring your site is easily visible can help minimize any negative results about your brand.
- **Links are valuable.** Any online marketing, public relations, or social media effort generally includes links back to the site. These links can be a valuable acquisition channel. Relevant links can also be valuable for helping search engines understand the value and context of the page.

Marketing, social media, and public relations can help your link profile considerably. Use social media to spread awareness about your great content, and you're likely to get bloggers to pick up on it and write about you. Once your PR team understands the importance of search and links, the team will do its part to make search acquisition effective by linking to specific pages (rather than just the home page) with descriptive anchor text in its press releases to increase the chances that news outlets will use those links and anchor text.

Market Research and Product Development

We've already seen just how valuable search data can be for market research, product development, and audience analysis. From an organizational standpoint, determine how use of search data can effectively be integrated into existing processes. This may be as easy as simply getting departments to share data. If the advertising department is already doing keyword research for paid search campaigns, it may be able to just share its findings with product development. If you are not currently using search data, user research, market research, or other departments you may need to learn how best to do keyword research and incorporate searcher personas into existing audience analysis and market research.

Metrics and Analytics

Use analytics data to augment search data and better understand your customers. (We'll talk more about analytics in Chapter 8.) You can learn what they're searching for that leads them to your site, what pages they find most useful, and what pages other sites find more valuable based on referral data. You can also use analytics to track your organic search efforts. Are you getting qualified traffic from the queries that you have targeted for your searcher personas? And are those searchers finding those pages useful?

Customer Support

We know that, as user behavior changes, more customers will turn to online support mechanisms. Customer support can take advantage of search in a number of ways including:

- Using search data to find out what problems customers are having and what they're searching for.
- Ensuring that searches for frequently asked questions bring up relevant answers from the company.
- Reaching out to any disgruntled customers who have posted negative information about the company (generally findable by doing brand searches).

Chapter 6 Checklist: Integrating Search into an Organization

Web architecture

☐ Web development and IT should build sites to be search-engine friendly (described in Chapter 7).
☐ Upper management should support a development lifecycle that includes time for incorporating search best practices.
☐ The site infrastructure should easily allow for content updates without code changes.
☐ The site should have useful site architecture with little duplication and clear navigation.
☐ Web pages should use standard HTML components, such as unique title tags, H1 tags and unique meta descriptions.
☐ Web pages should be accessible and render well on devices such as screen readers and mobile browsers.

Strategic and content development

☐ Business, product, and marketing goals should incorporate search data and organic search acquisition.
☐ All content should use the language of the customer, not the organization.
☐ Customer support should use search data to learn about problems before they escalate.

(continued)

(continued)

Advertising and marketing initiatives

❏ All offline campaigns should include requirements for brand visibility in organic search.
❏ Agencies should be given search-friendliness as a requirement for Web design or advertising campaigns.
❏ PR should understand the value of external links and ensure press releases are crafted to generate these effectively.

Checklist for Hiring an In-House SEO

❏ Project management experience.
❏ Ability to collaborate and work well with cross-functional teams.
❏ Good understanding of usability, conversion funnels, Web analytics, Web design, and information architecture design.
❏ Experience working with Web developers and firm understanding of technical requirements of organic search.
❏ Good writing skills and competent HTML skills.
❏ A similar approach and philosophy about organic search as yours.

Checklist for Hiring an Organic Search Agency

❏ Avoid firms that promise specific rankings.
❏ Avoid firms that provide rankings reports as a main deliverable.
❏ Avoid firms that don't disclose to you what actions they are taking on your behalf and what changes they are making to your site.
❏ Avoid firms that don't disclose their methods for link building or that perform link building by buying links or via link

exchange campaigns rather than by building long-term valuable content or engaging with the community.

☐ Ensure the firm has experience working with paid search agencies (if your organization uses paid search), Web developers and designers.

☐ Ensure the firm has a good understanding of usability, conversion funnels, Web analytics, Web design, and information architecture design.

☐ Ask about the firm's approach to organic search acquisition. It should align well with your company's philosophy and goals.

☐ Ask how the firm feels about Google's Webmaster guidelines.

☐ Evaluate the firm against Google's search engine optimization agency recommendations.[11]

CHAPTER

Working with Developers

How to Turn Business Strategy into Tech Speak

As noted in Chapter 6, a site's technical infrastructure is a vital part of search acquisition. If the search engine bots can't crawl and extract content from a site's pages, that site has little chance of ranking well in search engines for relevant queries. In addition, changing a site's content management system or server setup, merging sites after an acquisition, building micro sites and other common activities can greatly impact search acquisition.

Web developers should understand the principles of searchability and build them into the infrastructure and should have a set of best practices for modifying that infrastructure and troubleshooting problems. This chapter provides an overview of the technical issues involved with search acquisition. (You can find more detailed discussion at marketing intheageofgoogle.com.) You can use this chapter either to give directly to your Web developers, or if you're interested in the technical details, it can help you better understand the technical issues so you can have productive conversations with the development team about how best to build search best practices into the development process.

In order for search best practices to be successfully implemented in Web development, the development team needs executive support.

This means the developers need to be given the training to expand their core skill set into understanding how to make Web infrastructure searchable, they need time to test searchability in addition to functionality, and they need to be provided context about why they are being asked to make changes. Web developers know how to make sites functional and might be suspicious if you ask them to make changes which don't seem to improve functionality. But if you explain that both 301 and 302 redirects transfer the visitor from one page to another, only a 301 tells search engines to index the new page instead of the old one, you'll get the developers on your side much more quickly.

As noted in Chapter 5, the path to a site being found in search engines includes crawling, indexing, and ranking. Below are some more technical details on each of these components.

Crawling

The crawling process consists of several components. First, search engines have to learn about the pages. Then, they need to have enough time during the period they've allocated to the site to crawl those pages. Finally, they have to be able to technically access the pages.

Discovery

The first step in crawling is discovery. How does the engine find out about pages on the Web? Generally, this happens in one of the following ways:

- By finding links to the pages from other sites on the Web.
- By finding links to the pages from within your site.
- From an XML Site Map.

What's an XML Site Map?[1] It's a file in a particular format that contains a list of all the URLs on a site. Google, Yahoo!, and Microsoft Bing use this file to augment their discovery processes. Submitting a Site Map can help search engines know more comprehensively about your site. See sitemaps.com for more information.

Crawl Allocation

Search engine bots have resources to crawl every page on the Web and they are also mindful of not over crawling a site and causing an undue burden on the server. For these reasons, search engine bots only spend a limited period crawling each site. Factors that influence a more comprehensive crawl include:

- **Fast server response times.** If the server is slow to respond to requests, the search engine bots may slow down their crawl to ensure they aren't overloading the server.
- **Fast page load times.** The faster the pages load, the more of them search engines will likely be able to crawl during their allocated crawl period. You can monitor page load times for Google in Google Webmaster Tools. If you see a spike in page load times when you haven't made significant changes to your site (such as added substantial multimedia content), there may be a problem with the server (see Figure 7.1).
- **Unique content.** If much of the content appears to be duplicate or empty (this can happen, for instance, with directory sites that have regions, categories, or entries that don't yet have content), the search engine bot may stop crawling.
- **Accessible URLs.** URLs may be inaccessible to crawlers for a number of reasons, such as redirects are set up on the URLs that inadvertently create an infinite loop (so URLs redirect back and forth to each other) or that create a long redirect chain.[2] You can see a report of any URLs Google's bot couldn't access via Google Webmaster Central.[3]
- **Crawl efficiency.** If the crawler spends all its time on pages that you don't need to have indexed (such as registration pages and contact forms), less time will be available to crawl the pages you do want indexed. You can block content you don't want indexed using robots.txt.[4]
- **Server efficiency.** You can reduce the resources the search engine bot consumes per page by enabling compression and if-modified-since on the server. Compression serves pages to the bot in a compressed format and the if-modified-since response

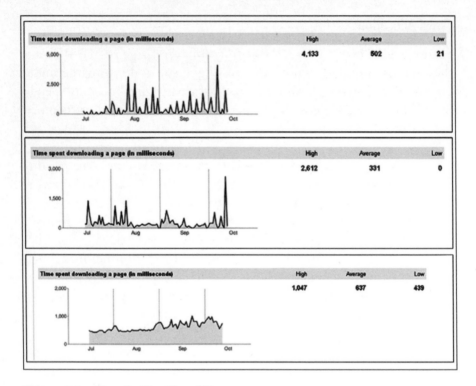

Figure 7.1   Google Site Crawl Report
Source: Google Webmaster Tools

returns a 304 (not modified) to the bot when it requests a page that hasn't changed since the last request rather than the entire contents of the page.[5]

- **Bot speed control.** You can slow down the crawl of Yahoo!'s and Microsoft's bot by using the crawl-delay setting in robots.txt.[6] If either of these bots seem to be crawling your site particularly slowly, check the robots.txt file to see if this entry exists. You can slow down Google's crawl of the site in Google Webmaster Tools. If Google is limiting its crawl because it's not sure if your server can handle a higher load, Google Webmaster Tools will present a "faster" option that you can specify as well (see Figure 7.2).

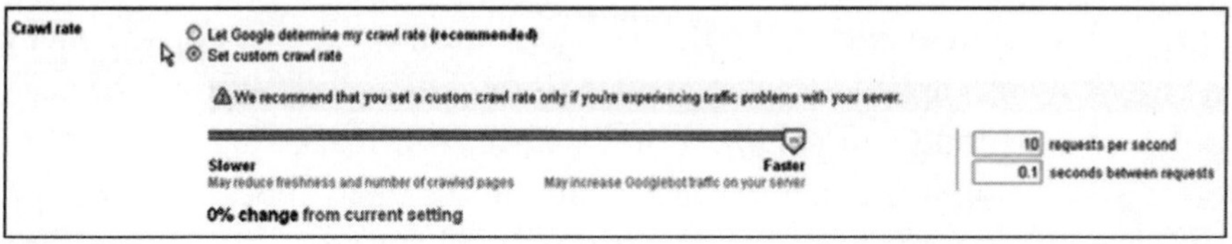

Figure 7.2   Google Webmaster Tools: Requesting a Faster Crawl

Source: Google Webmaster Tools

- **Canonicalization.** Canonicalization is the process of consolidating all duplicate URLs to one original, or "canonical," version.[7] If multiple URLs exist that all lead to the same page, then search engine bots may spend a considerable amount of time crawling the same page over and over via different URLs and not have time to get to unique pages. A number of methods exist for canonicalization of URLs.[8] The method to use depends on the canonicalization issue. Common issues include:

  $\longrightarrow$ **The www and non-www version of the site both resolve.** Ideally one version should redirect to the other.[9] For instance, when someone types in mysite.com, you can set the server to redirect to www.mysite.com. Without this redirect, an entire second copy of your site exists that search engines will try to crawl.

  $\longrightarrow$ **The URL structure has changed so content exists on both the old pages and the new pages.** In this situation, a redirect from the old pages to the new is generally the best way to go, particularly since it helps visitors to the old pages end up in the right place.

  $\longrightarrow$ **The URL structure generates infinite URLs.** With some URL implementations, any number of URLs may bring up the same page. For instance, on an e-commerce site, a product listing page may be available in different sort orders (ranked by lowest price, highest rated, etc.), but the content in each case is the same (just ordered differently). For instance, mystore.com/shoes.php?sort=lowest, mystore.com/shoes.php?sort=best, and mystore.com/shoes.php?sort=newest might bring up the same list of products. Another common way this happens is if the system is set up so that the marketing department or ad agency can append tracking codes to the URLs to keep track of marketing campaigns. For instance, the marketing department might send information about the new shoes page out in an e-mail newsletter with the URL mystore.com/shoes.php?source=email and might let bloggers know about the new shoes page, hoping they'll blog about it with the URL, mystore.com/shoes.php?source= blog. Both of these URLs bring up the same page. Session IDs appended to URLs can also cause infinite URL issues. If possible, store session information in cookies (and make sure those visitors who don't have cookie support—such as search engine bots—can access the site).

When a crawler detects that a page can load from infinite parameters, it may stop crawling that site to avoid being caught in what's known as a "spider trap." Another problem with this type of structure is that since the crawler has limited resources to spend on a site, time spent crawling the same page over and over from different URLs means that less time is available for crawling unique pages. In this situation, the canonical meta attribute[10] or the Google Webmaster Tools parameter handling tool[11] are good options.

$\longrightarrow$ **Pages are blocked by the robots exclusion protocol.**[12] The robots exclusion protocol enables you to block search engines from crawling parts of your entire site via either a robots.txt file located at the root of your site or via a meta tag on the source code of your pages. Many valid uses of this protocol exist, but it's easy to mistakenly block search engine bots from pages you do want to be indexed. If you find that your site isn't indexed as well as you'd like, check that the bots aren't accidentally being blocked out.

Indexing

Once a search engine bot has crawled a page, it attempts to store the contents of that page in the search engine index. Common reasons a search engine may not store the contents of a page include:

- **Incorrectly implemented redirects.** Most of the time, when you move content, you are moving it permanently. In those cases, implement redirects using the 301 HTTP status code. This code signifies that the change is permanent. Commonly, redirects default to the 302 HTTP status code, which signifies that the change is temporary. From a search engine perspective, this difference is important because if you've moved content (for instance, when changing domains or URL structure) you want the search engines to replace the old URLs with the new ones in the index. If possible, avoid JavaScript and Meta refresh redirects.

- **The content is locked behind registration.** If you require registration to view your content, search engine bots can't access it. A number of options exist for balancing search acquisition needs and registration requirements. For instance, you can provide abstracts of content outside of registration or you can participate in Google's First Click Free program.[13] This is discussed further at marketingintheageofgoogle.com.

- **The content is hidden in Flash or Silverlight.** Search engines have gotten better at crawling Flash pages, but a number of problems remain. You can find a list of resources on making Flash accessible to search engines at marketingintheageofgoogle.com.

- **The content is blocked by AJAX or JavaScript.** As with Flash, search engines are getting better at crawling other types of rich content such as AJAX and JavaScript, but only if developers implement these technologies in a search-friendly way. This type of implementation not only makes the content more accessible to crawling, it also makes it more accessible to visitors on mobile phones, screen readers, and older browsers. You can find a list of resources on making JavaScript accessible to search engines at marketingintheageofgoogle.com.

- **Little extractable text is available.** If the pages are full of video and images, search engines have little text with which to understand what those pages are about. At their core, we're still dealing with text-based search engines that return pages based on a searcher's text-based query. There are a number of ways you can ensure search engines can have some information about multi-media on your pages, such as images and videos:

$\longrightarrow$ **Images**[14]—Major search engines such as Google continue to be, at their cores, text based. They can't understand images without textual content. To ensure your site's images can be properly indexed and ranked by search engines, use descriptive ALT text, make image filenames descriptive (for instance, yellow-goldfish.jpg rather than image123.jpg), use descriptive text around the image (in captions, headings, and titles), and use high resolution, high quality images whenever possible. Be cautious about using images for navigation and avoid putting text into images.

$\longrightarrow$ **Video**—YouTube is the second largest search engine in the United States.[15] In August 2009, 40 percent of all online videos viewed in the United States were seen on YouTube. Your best bet for ensuring your video can be found may be to simply host it on YouTube. If you host it elsewhere, ensure the host is feeding Google a Video Site Map.[16] You should also provide transcripts, if possible, and use descriptive headings and descriptions for your videos.

• **Multiple sets of content associated with a single URL.** If the site is set up so that the URL doesn't change when the content changes or based on a single URL rather than allowing different users to be served regional content based on where they're located, search engines will only see one version of that URL. This often happens when the page is dynamically generated based on a visitor's location, for instance. A better strategy is to redirect to a separate URL with that regional content. For instance, local.com has a dynamically generated home page with local business information. Because the URL is the same no matter what content is loaded into the page, Google has indexed this URL with content from Mountain View, CA (where many Google bot computers crawl from) (see Figure 7.3).

Local.com could avoid this issue by redirecting the visitor to a URL such as local.com/mountain-view-ca or mountain-view-ca.local.com and displaying the local content there.

Figure 7.3   All Regional Content Should Load on Unique URLs

Source: Local.com

Ranking

As we've seen throughout this book, ranking is based on what pages search engines have calculated to be most relevant to what they have determined the searcher is looking for. You can't influence how the engines interpret searcher intent, but you can ensure your pages are as relevant as possible for target queries. The bottom line, of course, is to understand your customers and what they are looking for and provide exactly that. But on a more tactical level, relevance is based in large part on your site's content and on external links. We discussed both content and links in Chapter 6, but below are technical implementation details about the content.

Page Components

Content Architecture, on page 145, talked about the importance of including primary keywords in the page components. These components include page titles, meta descriptions, and heading tags, as described below. Key to making this work within an organization is ensuring that these components can be easily changed without requiring code change or launch. The content management system or other mechanism for building content should enable marketers, content writers, and others to easily change this text.

Page titles—This is what's contained in the <title> element in the source code and appears in the browser title bar. This text is important because it's what appears as the default title of a bookmark and generally is the title of the page in the search results. When possible, this tag should be formatted as follows:

Most important keyword in compelling phrase + Brand

For instance,

How to Rollerblade—eHow Videos

In the search results in Figure 7.4 [how to rollerblade], the first two results have titles that do a good job of describing what the page is about and the context (the site that the page is on). The third result is less trustworthy because the branding is unclear and the result below the videos is both missing branding and doesn't include the main keywords I was searching for. (This doesn't mean that this fourth result, "How to learn to rollerblade in a safe way," is poor phrasing. The site owners may have determined that "how to learn" and "safe" were crucial for attracting their target audience. And in fact, a search for [how to learn to

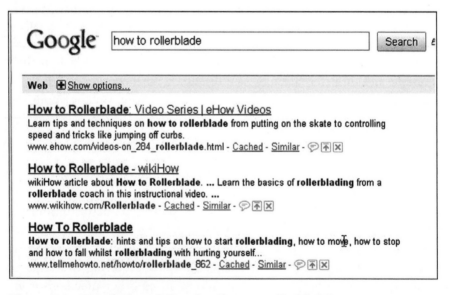

Figure 7.4   Google Search Results: [how to rollerblade]
Source: Google Search Results

rollerblade] brings them up first.) Each page should have a unique title that focuses on the core topic for that page. The page title is likely the most important element on the page.

Meta description—The meta description attribute is contained in the page's source code and is often used as the description below the title in the search results.[17] This is your chance to provide a targeted marketing message to engage with potential customers. It should be unique to each page and should give context to the content of the page. Since the search results description real estate is limited be concise, provide a compelling value proposition for the page, and use the primary keywords you've chosen for the page. However, don't make the mistake of repeating the keywords, as this doesn't help ranking and can make the result look spammy. The words from the search query are bolded, which can draw the searcher's attention to your listing.

Search engines don't always use the meta description in the results. Based on the query, other text from the page may be deemed more relevant and may be shown instead. Search engines will also pull this text from elsewhere if the meta description text is too short.

Let's take a closer look at the [how to rollerblade] results.

The first result (from ehow.com) has an informative and compelling description. From the source code, we can see that this text comes directly from the meta description (see Figure 7.5).

The second result (wikihow.com) isn't quite as succinct or compelling.

It wastes valuable real estate by repeating the brand (which is already evident in the title), it is cluttered by ellipses and unfinished phrases, and it has casing issues. Looking at the source code, the problem is clear. While the meta description tag exists, it's too short for Google to consider it to be meaningful (see Figure 7.6). Therefore, Google

```
<meta name="description" content="Learn tips and
techniques on how to rollerblade from putting on the
skate to controlling speed and tricks like jumping off
curbs." />
```

Figure 7.5 A Compelling Meta Description

Source: Ehow.com'

```
<meta name="description" content="wikiHow article about
How to Rollerblade." />
```

Figure 7.6   A Less Compelling Meta Description
Source: Wikihow.com

has used it, has added content from other places on the page to construct a search results description. The repeated brand and use of mixed casing comes directly from the site-provided meta description.

The title of the page ("How to Rollerblade") likely was dynamically added to the meta description. This practice can be a scalable way to create unique meta descriptions for a large number of pages, but when implementing a technical solution like this, review the finished product. In this case, the description could be made significantly better for users by simply adding a line of code that lowercases the words when inserted into the middle of a sentence.

Headings—Whenever possible, pages should use semantic markup for clearer meaning for both search engines and devices such as screen readers. Headings are marked up in HTML using <H> tags. Generally a page has one <H1> tag, a few more <H2> tags, and so on, much like numbering an outline. Headings are important for a couple of reasons. Search engines *can* use the text in them to determine relevance, although how much weight they're given may vary. More importantly, a descriptive heading can provide context to searchers to let them know they're on the correct page. As you recall from the page content phase of the searcher workflow, this context is important for anchoring the visitor and ensuring they don't bounce back to the search results.

Content—Each page should contain enough text to provide valuable information to the visitor. This text should use the language of the visitor (based on keyword research).

Syndication

There are good reasons for syndicating content. Syndication can bring traffic, exposure, and sales.

If you're a blogger, you might syndicate your posts to get wider distribution. If your posts are seen by a bigger audience, you might gain some of those readers for yourself. If your site provides authoritative resources, you might have a partnership with other sites that want to include that content. And if you sell products, you might provide affiliates with content feeds, which in turn brings in additional revenue.

But What Should Rank? But from a search engine perspective, syndication can cause a bit of a conundrum. If what you wrote is a relevant result for a search, the search engine wants to show it to the searcher—but not show it twice (or three times, or maybe even a thousand times in the case of an affiliate feed). And that makes sense. If you're searching for something, you don't want multiple results that all lead to the same content even if that content is on different sites.

So what's a search engine to do?

Search engines generally identify duplicate results and filter out all but one. They have lots of ways to decide which version to show. They try to figure out which one is the "original" by looking at things like which version was published first and which has the most links pointing to it.

Your content may appear on other sites at times other than when you syndicated it (such as when your RSS feed has been scraped), and search engines try to account for that too by looking at things like which site is more authoritative.

How Can You Make Sure Your Site Ranks First? So what do I suggest you do if you're syndicating content but want your original version to rank above the syndicated ones?

- Create a different version of the content to syndicate than what you write for your own site. This method works best for things like product affiliate feeds. I don't think it works as well for things like blog posts or other types of articles. Instead, you could do something like write a high level summary article for syndication and a blog post with details about that topic for your own site.
- Always include absolute links back to your own site in the body of the article. This is particularly helpful when your content is scraped.
- Ask your syndication partners to block their version of your article (via robots.txt or a robots meta tag or the re=canonical attribute that points back to your site). If you are able to, put together a syndication agreement that states they get your content as a benefit for their readers, not as a way to acquire search traffic for that content; then you can keep control of ranking for what you've written and they can provide a benefit to their audience.

Maintain control. If search is not yet a large acquisition channel for your site, then you may not mind if another site ranks for your material as you may get more traffic from the syndicated site (so make sure you at least have a link back to your site). But as your site starts to stand on its own and search traffic starts growing, you will want to have more control. So think of your longer term strategy when you negotiate syndication partnerships and don't give up all of the control of the content you work so hard to create to others.

Content That's Not Unique

Syndication isn't the only instance in which duplication can cause ranking problems. Another common issue comes up with e-commerce sites. Many companies use manufacturer databases or product feeds to describe products for sale. After all, it may not be reasonable to write unique product descriptions for millions of products. But remember that thousands of other sites may be using those identical product descriptions. How do search engines decide which to rank?

You can try to outrank every site that uses the same product descriptions, but a better strategy may be to add unique value on top of that content. For instance, you can aggregate information to provide comparisons between products or brands. You can also enable user-generated content so visitors can provide reviews, ratings, and comments. This information adds value to the page beyond the boilerplate description.

Search Engine Tools for Webmasters

All three major search engines have tools and educational resources for site owners. These tools provide great diagnostic reports, as well as statistics, and ways of providing input to the engines. You can find these tools at:

Google Webmaster Central: google.com/webmasters
Microsoft Bing Webmaster Center: webmaster.bing.com
Yahoo! Site Explorer: siteexplorer.search.yahoo.com

Chapter 7: Web Development Checklist

Crawlability

❏ Every page on the site should have at least one internal link. The site should be easy to browse.

❏ Every page on the site should be listed in an XML Site Map, which should then be submitted to the major search engines.

❏ The site should be well-linked throughout the Web.

❏ Each URL should be accessible and not create infinite versions or redirect loops.

❏ Multiple versions of a URL shouldn't resolve to the same content and if they do, canonicalization techniques should be implemented.

❏ If the URL structure changes, implement 301 redirects from the old URLs to the new ones.

❏ Ensure the site or parts of it aren't inadvertently blocked with robots.txt.

❏ Ensure you are using the tools from the major search engines to be alerted of any crawling issues.

Crawl Efficiency

❏ The server should quickly respond to requests.

❏ Pages should load quickly.

❏ Each page should contain substantial unique content.

❏ The server should use compression and should return a 304 not modified response when content hasn't changed.

Indexability

❏ Ensure redirects are implemented via 301 and not 302 (or through JavaScript).

❏ Ensure all content you want indexed is available and not blocked behind a login.

❏ Ensure all content is extractable. If the site is implemented using Flash, Silverlight, JavaScript, or AJAX, ensure those technologies are implemented in a search-friendly way.

(continued)

(*continued*)

❏ Ensure all multimedia such as images and video are implemented in a search-friendly way.
❏ The same URL shouldn't serve up different content. For instance, if you want to serve different content based on region, redirect visitors to a separate URL for each set of content.
❏ Ensure each page's title element, meta description tag, and H1 contain the vital keywords for the page and include them in a compelling way for visitors.
❏ Ensure that all content is unique across the Web. If you syndicate content or publish content that's syndicated, ensure you have a strategy to avoid duplication issues.

How to Cut Through the Data and Get the Actionable Metrics You Need

There's no shortage of analytics data available. In fact, that tends to be the problem. So much data exists that it can be difficult to figure out what's important and actionable. Particularly from a search perspective, the key is remembering those goals you defined when building searcher personas. What metrics give you insight into how well you are reaching those goals? And just as importantly, what can you do with the data you're tracking?

Conversion Rates

Businesses are finally starting to break out conversion rates from search. But too many of them start and end there. At a recent tech event in Seattle, the CEO from Redfin noted that their conversion rate from search is low.[1] But "from search" is like calculating a conversion rate from TV ads with no interest in whether the commercials aired during a Friday night monster truck rally or a Saturday morning cartoon, or like only tracking the conversion rate for "advertising," when that might include TV, radio, print, and online.

Conversion rate is absolutely important to understanding how well a site is performing, but it's much more actionable when viewed by acquisition segment. Even better is if you can tie visitors to future behavior. Do visitors who come in through message boards talking about eco-friendly materials read an average of three articles on the site, share those links on two social media sites, which in turn bring in 12 visitors who convert?

Avinash Kaushik, Google's analytics evangelist and author of *Web Analytics: An Hour a Day* and *Web Analytics 2.0: The Art of Online Accountability and Science of Customer Centricity*, suggests rolling all conversion data into one metric: task completion rate by primary purpose.[2]

He suggests finding out the core reasons why visitors come to your site. One way is to display an optional survey that asks, "why are you visiting the site today," and then determining if each visitor segment was able to complete the task. Another way is to simply ask.

He suggests that this metric is more valuable than conversion rate to your business goal (selling something, etc.) because not all visitors are there for that purpose and, therefore, will never convert in the way you are measuring.[3] Some percentage of visitors is looking for company information, product support, or other information. You want to find out all the reasons that bring visitors to your site and if you are meeting their needs. In some cases, understanding this can help increase satisfaction of existing customers and improve customer lifetime value; in other cases, this can help increase engagement of potential customers and improve the likelihood that they will return to purchase later. But, just as important, by segmenting those visitors who are not there to purchase today (or do whatever task is mapped to your conversion goal), you have better insight into how well you are converting those visitors who do have purchase intent.

And you have substantially better insight into how your Web site is failing your visitor needs.

Defining Goals

Define your goals before setting up metrics for your search acquisition strategy. When I ask people what their goals are for a particular site or page, I hear answers like "to rank well" and "to get more traffic."

But those aren't business goals. You only want to rank well so you can attract visitors to your site and you only want to attract visitors to your site if you have a reasonable chance of converting them.

What's Not Important

Look at most Web analytics and SEO reports and you'll see things like the following:

- Rankings reports that list hundreds of keywords and how the site ranks for them.
- Indexing reports that show the change in the number of indexed pages over time.
- Absolute traffic numbers.
- Overall percentage of traffic from organic search and overall conversion rate from organic search.
- Page views.
- Daily unique visitors.
- Top entry and exit pages.
- Visitor screen resolutions and browser versions.

But these numbers tell us little if anything about the performance of the site. Who are these visitors? What are they looking for? Are they the visitors we are trying to attract? Did we engage them?

Better metrics would focus on goals and actionable insights:

- What's the organic search traffic breakdown for query categories we are targeting and how are those visitors behaving on the site? (Are they converting? Engaging? Abandoning right away?)
- What query categories aren't performing as well as we'd like? Is the performance breakdown at the search result (resulting in lack of traffic for those queries to the site) or at the site level (resulting in early abandonment or low conversion rates)?
- What are the primary reasons visitors are coming to the site and what are their task completion rates?

- What referring links are bringing the most traffic and how well are those visitors performing on the site? If they're performing well, this may be an audience you should spent time cultivating.

The specific metrics that help you measure your business are unique to your site, but always evaluate them against the following:

- Do they give you insight into how well you are meeting your goals?
- Are they actionable? What will you do with this data?

Competitive Intelligence as a Benchmark to How Well You're Really Doing

Benchmarking data can be a valuable data point about how well you're really doing. It can help you know if an increase in search traffic is due to an overall trend of higher search volumes for your industry or is at the expense of your competition.

Having Actionable Analytics Data Is a Competitive Advantage

By some estimates, only 23 percent of sites have an analytics package installed, and only 1 percent are doing A/B or multivariate testing.[4] By simply having this data at hand, you're well ahead of most of your competition.

Attribution

Attribution issues make metrics even more complicated. As we've seen, searchers don't always follow a straight path from search to purchase. They not only may search for several different things (with subsequent queries triggered in part by results they saw in earlier queries), but may also search over more than one session. One study found that 56 percent of purchases occur in a search session later than the first one.[5] Another found that only 43 percent of purchasers make that purchase within an

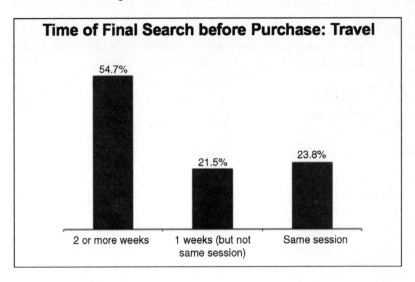

Figure 8.1 Travel Search Conversion
Source: DoubleClick

hour of the site visit. For some categories, the lag times can be substantial, such as shown below with a graph from a DoubleClick study (see Figure 8.1).

eBay, which we'll learn more about shortly, handles the attribution issue in its metrics by using cookie data to store visitor information and attributing a conversion to search if it happens within 24 hours. The numbers tell us that this method isn't perfect, but it's better than only attributing conversions at the point of searching.

In addition to the time lag element of attribution, there's the triggering element. We can see this in a hypothetical example for Volvo. In this example, we'll consider entering a zip code to find the nearest dealer a conversion (see Figure 8.2).

Looking at these hypothetical numbers separately, branded search converts significantly better than non-branded search or display ads. With display ads, 20,000 people saw the ad, but only 1,000 of those clicked on it; and of that 1,000, only 50 converted. But with branded search, 10,000 people clicked on the Volvo result after searching for it and 6,000 of them converted. In isolation, it seems clear that we should stop our display advertising spend, stop optimizing for non-branded searches, and put all of our energy toward branded search. Or should we?

	A	B	C
1	Entry Point	Monthly Volume	Conversion Rate
2	Display ads	1,000 visitors (20,000 impressions)	5%
3	Non-branded search	30,000 visitors	15%
4	Branded search	10,000 visitors	60%

Figure 8.2   Conversion Metrics from Multiple Channels

Let's take a closer look. In this example, 50,000 people did non-branded searches (such as fuel-efficient cars and safe cars). Of those 50,000, 30,000 visited the site and 30,000 x .15 converted, but all 50,000 saw the Volvo brand in the results. Of the 20,000 people who saw the display ad, only 1,000 clicked through to the site, but all 20,000 saw the Volvo brand.

One thousand of the people who saw the Volvo ad later searched for [Volvo] and clicked through to the site and 5,000 of the people who did non-branded searches and saw the Volvo result later searched for [Volvo] and clicked through to the site.

So without the display ads and non-branded search results, we'd be left with only 4,000 visitors. Study[6] after study[7] has found that most prepurchase activity involves generic terms and that brand searches tend to happen only close to purchase (see Figures 8.3 and 8.4).

Clearly the generic searches are providing insight into brands or the searchers would simply begin with brand searches. Many searches don't search for brands at all before purchasing.

But how do you track searcher behavior across multiple sessions? Several companies are trying to solve this problem. Some of them store information in a user's cookie when a display ad is served, for instance, and later can determine what users saw the display ad then later did searches that led those users to the site (and what those searches were). These technologies aren't able to tell when a searcher has seen an organic result and not clicked on it. (The only way to currently get organic impression information is via Google Webmaster Tools, and that data is only in aggregate, not per visitor).

You can track visitors by IP address as well, although this method isn't 100 percent reliable either, since many people search at work and

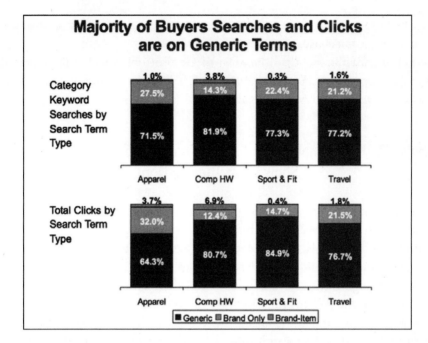

Figure 8.3   The Importance of Generic Searches
Source: DoubleClick

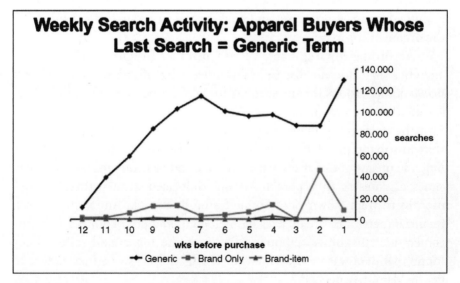

Figure 8.4   Generic Search Behavior
Source: DoubleClick

buy at home or search in one location and then e-mail their spouse the link for later purchase.

For more in-depth discussion of attribution in web analytics and possible approaches, See *Web Analytics 2.0: The Art of Online Accountability and Science of Customer Centricity* by Avinash Kaushik.

How eBay Uses Analytics to Inform What They Should Do, Not Just Show What They've Done

eBay has one of the largest Web sites in the world and, judging by the paid search ads served up with nearly every query, is one of the largest bidders on keywords. Between the paid search data about what people are searching for and what they click on and information about how visitors navigate the site, eBay has one of the largest data sets on user behavior of any site on the Web. A few short years ago, those at eBay threw most of that information away after only six months. In 2006, they realized they had a goldmine of data that could help them better understand their customers, build better buying and selling experiences, and improve eBay. Now, they protect that data vigilantly and have realigned business processes and goals to prioritize analytics throughout the organization.

According to Greg Fant, VP of Customer Insights and Marketing, analytics data doesn't just tell eBay how it has done; they tell what it *should* do. Decisions that used to take weeks of one person's opinion versus another are now data driven. The site's testing platform helps confirm the decisions. Using data to drive strategy was an organizational shift in solving problems that didn't come easily. But the benefits were huge. Fant says those at eBay used to be blind to problems but now they can see issues as they pop up. Issues that used to take three to four months to track down can now be found in a week. And shifting from financial metrics to site metrics has helped them better connect with customers and maximize happiness for both the buyer and seller. They found that data was so vital that they changed their site infrastructure to get the data they needed.[8]

Those at eBay are quick to stress that search and Web analytics data helps them with all decisions, not just marketing-related ones.

Both organic and paid search data helps them discern searcher intent, find patterns in queries, and learn broader classifications and interests than what they can get from just monitoring on-site behavior. They pay close attention to what queries searchers are pairing with the word "eBay." What problems are they having? What are they looking for eBay to provide? By identifying "silent sufferers," they can learn about issues and solve them before they become widespread pain points.

Segmenting by query type has helped those at eBay identify different loyalty points, learn about ways different segments are motivated, and begin to better understand the analytics holy grail that is customer lifetime value.

How has eBay been able to transition to a data-driven organization, build search data into product strategy, and break down data silos? It has been a long process. Those at eBay credit support from the top: board-level agreement led to an organizational shift and analytical platform from which to base decisions. And the rest of the company came on board through a common set of metrics and vision across the entire company. When everyone is working towards the same goal and is measuring the same things, sharing data becomes significantly easier. For eBay, that common metric is purchases per week. Analytics used to be spread out under multiple divisions. They've now centralized. They focus on data that's practical and actionable.

They go after low-hanging fruit for quick wins along the way while they work on longer-term initiatives such as new infrastructure and an A/B testing platform. They build some things on a separate infrastructure for faster implementation and less impact to the primary site. They prioritize (based, of course, on data). And they've built an in-house organic search team that is focused on understanding how Google crawls, indexes, and ranks. Dennis Goedegebuure, Senior Manager of SEO, has made it his mission to build a centralized organic search team and develop search-friendly best practices throughout the organization.

Fant talks about a new breed of data-driven marketers and leadership teams who are ushering eBay into a new era of audience analysis, market research, and product strategy. At eBay, everyone understands that the user experience often begins on Google, and they spend a lot of time working to understand what Google searchers are really looking for.

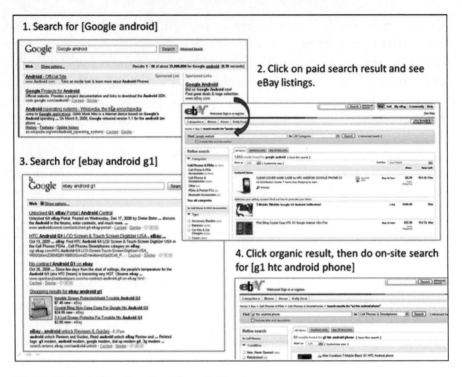

Figure 8.5   A Sample eBay Search Session

Source: Google Search Results and eBay

Both intent and attribution are issues that eBay spends a lot of time on. A sample customer interaction on eBay is shown in Figure 8.5.

In this example, the searcher initially looks for [Google Android] and clicks on eBay's paid search ad. This brings the searcher to an eBay page that lists items related to Google Android, including phones, phone covers, and chargers. The searcher later goes back to Google and this time remembers both that eBay had relevant information and that the previous search hadn't been specific enough to bring back only phones. So, the second search is for [eBay Android G1]. This time, the searcher clicks eBay's organic result and lands on another search results page that still isn't quite specific enough. The searcher then searches within eBay to better refine the results and ultimately clicks an item listing.

In this scenario, if eBay tracked only the search that led to the click on the item listing, they would know only that the visitor had searched for [G1 HTC Android phone]. Had they only followed the path back one level, they would know that being visible in organic results is important, but they wouldn't know that the paid search ad was important for branding and caused the searcher to include the word "eBay" in that search. By following the visitor all the way to the initial search, eBay knows that the word "Google" was initially an important component, dropped later only to make room for more specific keywords. The complete picture is much more helpful in formulating customer understanding than just the final query.

But this very common navigation path raises hard attribution questions. Who gets credit for the sale? Paid search? Organic search? Internal site search? In truth, they all contributed to the customer's path to conversion. Without any one of them, the sale may never have happened.

When eBay started revising their product pages based on user data such as this, traffic from search went down. eBay couldn't be more pleased. Why? Because eBay has higher quality, more descriptive pages in the search results, the quality of the traffic now is substantially better. Searchers who are genuinely interested in buying and selling are the ones clicking through the search results and visiting the site. And the pages they are visiting are the pages most likely to convert. eBay no longer has as much unqualified traffic to pages that have low conversion value. eBay has learned that traffic alone is meaningless. More traffic isn't necessarily better.

By incorporating search data throughout their organization, eBay makes better business decisions, builds more effective product strategy, connects more closely with customers, and knows about problems before they escalate. It has created a more efficient working relationship between teams, and ultimately, has increased purchases per week.

Can Software Accurately Calculate Attribution?

Enquisite[9] is a software company trying to address the issues of attribution and return on investment (ROI) metrics for organic search. It is building predictive modeling and analysis tools for all aspects of search analytics, including organic, paid, and referral links. It keeps track of traffic differences between search engines, generates long-tail traffic reports, and provides insights into business-to-business traffic. It is using search and analytics data to help companies understand user behavior, what topics and products perform best, and to build rollout dashboards that provide concrete measurements at a glance.

Can Enquisite help eBay with its attribution problem? Maybe. Richard Zwicky, Enquisite founder, says those at Enquisite use persistent and session-based cookies to understand the full visitor path, not simply the last click. They know what the visitor searched for before the last search, and they can weigh the value of the clicks themselves. They are also attempting to relate value across channels. Just how valuable was that paid search ad in influencing the searcher's decision to later do a brand search and ultimately purchase from eBay?

ClearSaleing is also tackling the attribution issue. Their *Attribution Management Buyer's Guide* outlines their approach to calculating attribution across online channels, including both paid and organic search.[10] As they note,

> . . . *many conversions are the result of multiple forms of advertising. For example, a banner impression leads someone [to] click on a paid search ad, then an organic search, and then they convert. If the solution you're using is only able to capture paid search, it would be oblivious to the fact that the banner impression is what introduced that person to your brand, and that the organic listing is what eventually closed the deal.*[11]

What About Offline Attribution?

Of course, ideally, attribution tracking would include offline channels as well (both for bringing in customers and for the conversion). How can you track a billboard that leads to a search that leads to a sale, such as the case of the movie 2012? What about a search that leads to a phone call that leads to a sale? We know that television advertising triggers search,[12] and we know that searches are often the first step to offline purchases,[13] but can we track that?

A number of at least partial solutions exist for offline attribution, but the key is understanding that a relationship exists, sharing data between departments, and devoting resources to learning how these relationships work for your customer base.

For instance, dynamic number insertion[14] can help track phone calls based on different search ads. You can use a different phone number online than in printed materials so that you can track online and offline channels. You can provide online coupons to be used for offline purchases. You can even display different coupons based on what search led the visitor to the page. At a more basic level, you can track the change in offline purchases as your site becomes more visible in organic search (noting other factors, such as advertising and seasonal fluctuations that may impact this).

The Trouble with Data

The trouble with data on the Web is that it's impossible to measure with absolute accuracy.[15] This is true of data everywhere, of course; it's just more measurable on the Web. Cities hire car counting firms to track how busy intersections are to make decisions about new traffic signals, and, although it's likely the counters miss a few cars here and there, the city can still be fairly confident in the conclusions. We track how many people are watching particular television shows by relying on a sampling of viewers to accurately log their viewing habits. They don't, of course, but it's still the best signal we've got. With Web analytics data, it's much easier to tell just how far off the numbers are. If you run two Web analytics programs on your site in parallel (and many sites do), you will come up with two sets of data that can never be reconciled. But that's OK. Rather than spend your time trying to reconcile them, just know that they are about as accurate as Nielson data or car counting and can be used for overall trends and measurements, if not exact counts.

The Value of an Experienced In-House Web Analytics Expert

Accurate, actionable data is critical in today's online environment. And with so much data available—much of it confusing and not actionable—the best way to cut through to what really matters is to ensure you have a skilled Web analytics expert on staff who can cull through the hundreds of data points and give you the top five metrics that show you how the business is going and help you make business decisions.

Avinash Kaushik, wrote on his blog about the top things to look for in a Web analytics manager. They include:

- **Has passion:** "You have to love the Web, you have to love its life changing power, you have to believe that at some level you, yes you, have the power to change people's lives by killing reports that show, in 8 font, conversion and visitors stats and replacing them with analysis that will fundamentally improve the experiences of your customers and ease their stress."
- **Loves change:** "The Web changes and grows and morphs like an alien being. You just got used to prefetching and here is Google trying to guess searcher intent (and now "personalized search" where even your awesome organic listing might not result in your being number one) and then come RIAs and Ajax and then will come something else and, like a tidal wave, it keeps coming. Ask for one thing they know of that will mess up the analytics world in the next 180 days. If they have an answer, you have a winner."
- **Questions data:** "The core problem with all the tools today is that they rely on data that usually tells you little. [Good analysts] question the data and analysis and bring a new and different perspective and can overcome cool recommendations from the latest consultant."
- **Believes in customer-driven innovation:** "True innovation and sustainable competitive advantage will [often] come from actions that are Customer Driven. What this translates into is a Manager who has had exposure to Testing and Usability and Surveys and Site Visits and Field Studies or Market Research . . . someone who can bring to bear their experience to find the right ways for you to apply the power of analytics and research to find the right answers for your customers."

Data is tricky. You need to make sure the underlying data is solid so you know you can trust your conclusions. You need to measure the right things. And you need to focus your investments on analyzing data that's actionable. A great Web analytics manager, particularly one who understands that all acquisition channels bring the same customers, can ensure that you are looking at the right data and taking full advantage of it.

CHAPTER 9

Social Media and Search

We've seen how valuable it can be to appear in search results when searchers are looking for what you have to offer, and we've seen the important role that links play in helping your site rank well. We've also seen how keyword research can provide insight into how your potential customers are thinking about your brand, your industry, and your competition.

Social media can help on all of these fronts, working as a brand amplifier and customer support extension to deepen engagement with your customers.

What Is Social Media?

Lately, when people hear the term "social media" they tend to think of the fairly new developments of sites such as Facebook and MySpace, but in reality, social media has been around as long as we have been social and have used media. Letters to the editor in traditional print newspapers are an example of social media.

Online social media, in turn, has been around as long as we've been online. Before what we now know as the World Wide Web, people were connecting all over the world via "bulletin board systems" (BBS) and later in chat rooms on platforms such as Prodigy and CompuServe. Today, even multi-player online games such as World of Warcraft are social media—they are yet another way that people connect online. Online social media, as defined for the purposes of this book, includes:

- **Discussion sites**—these include general and topic specific message boards.
- **Content sharing sites**—these include any sites that enable users to share what they've created with each other, such as photo sharing sites (like Flickr), blogging platforms (like Blogger and Wordpress), and micro blogging platforms (like Twitter). For the purpose of this book, social bookmarking sites, such as Delicious and Digg fit into this category as well.
- **Social networking sites**—these include places that exist specifically to facilitate connections between people. For instance, Facebook began as a way for college students to stay in touch and now enables friends, families, and colleagues to share contact information, photos, and all variety of details about their lives.
- **Review sites**—these are most often seen as stand-alone sites, such as TripAdvisor, which focuses on sharing information about travel, but can also be part of larger sites. Amazon, for instance, is an e-commerce site, but has a large social review component.

Of course, you can see that many of these categories overlap. Digg and Slashdot both enable users to share content they've found, as well as discuss that content with each other. Flickr is primarily focused on sharing photos, but users often get into lengthy discussions and form groups around particular topics.

Involvement in social media can be beneficial to companies for a number of reasons, but for this book, we'll focus on how social media can benefit you as it relates to search.[1]

Other Types of Media

Being involved in other types of media (such as press) can be beneficial from a search perspective for many of the same reasons as social media, so it's included in this chapter as well. Other types of online media include online newspapers and magazines (and blogs as well, although those can also be considered a type of content-sharing social media), press releases, syndicated or original articles published on sites other than your own, and interviews (given to traditional press or others).

Being Visible in Search Results

As we've seen, if your brand doesn't appear in search results for queries related to your industry or product, searchers are unlikely to consider you and you'll often lose that potential customer to the competition. One way to appear in search results, of course, is by ensuring your own site appears, but social media gives you nearly infinite opportunity to show up for any number of queries that use language you may not even realize your customers are using.

The most important thing to realize is that potential customers are looking for authenticity. Attempts to blanket social media sites with positive mentions of your brand are likely to backfire. Much better tactics include:

- Ensuring you have a voice in places your customers are talking about you.
- Facilitating discussions online with your customers and potential customers.
- Providing useful and targeted content (in the form of press releases or other resources, articles, and interviews) to interested content creators. (This means not sending out press releases to an untargeted mass distribution list, but identifying those reporters and bloggers who care about your industry and sending them customized e-mail that describes why you think they're interested and what you're willing to provide to them.)

Monitor the likely places where people could be talking about your brand, product or industry (you can do this manually or by engaging a service), and build up a brand presence in those locations. Contribute to the conversation whenever useful (by providing additional resources or information, clarifying details, and fixing problems).

The trick is to be helpful rather than overly promotional. Keep in mind that people aren't spending time on these sites to be marketed to. However, they are interested in your product or industry and welcome solutions to their problems, inside information, and avenues for providing feedback.

How does this relate to search? Say you run a printer business and you've started contributing to printer forums in threads where users have been troubleshooting issues. For instance, in one thread, a customer who owns the Acme 1250 color inkjet may be asking if he can print photos and, if so, how he can produce the best prints. You reply with details on the best paper to use, the settings to configure, and how to change the options for 3×5 versus 5×7 prints. The customer is ecstatic and tells all his friends about the great service he received.

In the days before the Web, he may have simply asked his friends or the local print shop for help and your company would never have had the opportunity to help him. Or, he may have called your 800-number, gotten great service, and told all his friends.

The difference now is that at least 10,000 people a month are searching for information on how to print photos.[2] If the discussion thread that you've provided such useful information for appears on the first page of results for these queries, you've help open a whole new avenue for customer acquisition. As a bonus, the discussion will be slightly different on each site. Some people will ask how to print digital photos, others will wonder how to print pictures, and still others will ask if they can print pictures from their digital camera. If you run a printer business, you'll want to include a page on your Web site that describes digital printing, but it's unlikely you'll be able to account for all the various ways people will search for the topic. By contributing to discussions throughout the Web that ask questions about digital printing, you'll have many more opportunities to rank for related queries, no matter how they're worded.

These discussions may also help your brand be seen by people doing more generic searches, such as those researching what type of printer to buy. Each month, 7.5 million searches occur about printers, and nearly half a million of those searches are more specifically about digital printing.[3] If even a small subset of those searchers are in the market for a printer and see a discussion in which your brand has shown itself to be helpful and responsive to customer needs, you've gained an advantage in competitive analysis those searchers may be doing.

The Synergies of Search and Social Media and PR

Consider that the PR you do or social media you become involved with will live well beyond the initial publication or post.

For instance, consider a restaurant. In years past, a positive write up in a newspaper or magazine might result in filled tables the next weekend. One neighbor recounting a delicious meal to another neighbor while walking the dog might get the restaurant an additional reservation that week.

But consider how things have changed with our increasing reliance on search. I'm writing this from Bologna, Italy, and a little earlier today, I decided to venture into the town for lunch. But how do I pick a location in a city famous for its food? With the help of search, of course. Searching for [best place to have lunch in Bologna Italy] brought up an article in *The Guardian* called "24 hours in Bologna: Foodie Heaven" that listed five promising choices. These five restaurants didn't only get the lift in visibility during the week that article initially ran in the paper and only among regular readers. The article was written in 2000 and was still showing up on the first page of search results. One positive review has been sending customers to these restaurants for nine years (and counting). Also in the top five was a discussion of Bologna restaurants from the message board Chowhound.com (see Figure 9.1).

Businesses spend a great deal of time and energy on getting that one positive mention in mainstream press, that one good interview, that one well-placed signal of support, even though that publicity can be fleeting and untargeted. But let PR and social media work for you in search and capture a far more receptive audience (one who is specifically searching for what you offer) for years to come.

Online Reputation Management

If you've been around for any length of time, it's likely that someone out there doesn't like you. If you're absent from search, it could be your detractor's site that shows up when potential customers search for you.

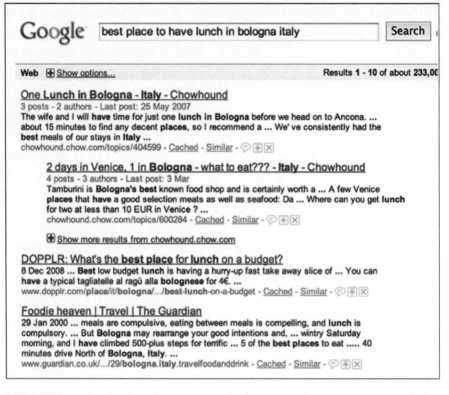

Figure 9.1   Google Search Results: [places to have lunch in Bologna Italy]

Source: Google Search Results

Generally, there's not much you can do about this. Search engines such as Google merely index the Web and don't evaluate the contents for lack of criticism or even truthfulness.

But if your brand has positive mentions throughout the Web via social media sites, press, and other avenues, those mentions could rank highly and push negative mentions of your brand lower in the search results, decreasing chances that searchers even see them.

Lessons from the TSA

We can see this in action with an incident involving the U.S. Transportation Security Administration (TSA). A mom wrote a scathing blog post in which she accused the TSA of taking her baby from her and walking away with him during a routine security check at the airport. The story caught fire and the Google search results for [TSA takes baby] were filled with recounting of the story. The TSA responded the very same day on their blog with video footage showing that in fact, the baby was never separated from the mother and sat in his stroller beside her during the screening. The content of the Google search results quickly changed. A search for [TSA takes baby] became filled with stories about the TSA blog post and the original stories included updates with the TSA's side of the story (see Figure 9.2).

What could have been a public relations disaster for the TSA was quickly averted and anyone searching for information on the story was presented with both sides. The TSA didn't just stop there. They monitored the story and updated their post with answers to questions and additional video footage.

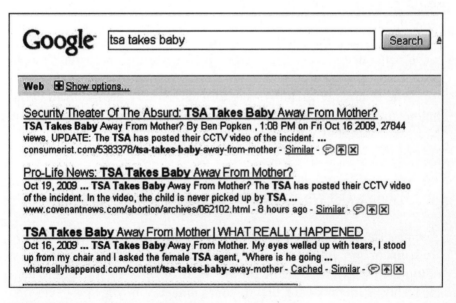

Figure 9.2 Google Search Results: [tsa takes baby]

Source: Google Search Results

Helping Your Company Site to Rank Well

As mentioned on page 112, relevant external links to your site are an important factor in how search engines decide how to order search results. By raising awareness about your brand and product on a site such as Digg or Flickr, you increase the chances that others will mention (and link to) you in blogs, forums, and social networking sites. The key is targeting an interested audience. While Digg has a large audience, it may not include very many people who are interested in your industry and who are likely to, in turn, blog about it.

Market Research

In Chapter 2, you learned about how to use keyword research tools to find out what your potential customers are most interested in. You can also use search itself to find out what they're saying about you, your competition, and your industry. The advantage of adding social media search to your market research toolset is that you'll get near real-time information that can help alert you to any upcoming public relations issues, get a head start on the competition about coming trends, and get much richer detail than a list of generated keywords from search data can provide.

You're already keeping track of where you're being talked about online and becoming involved in the conversation as described above. Now you can simply take the next step and use this information for market research.

Finding Out Where People Are Talking about You Online

The first step to finding out where the conversations of interest to you are happening online is compiling a list of sources. Next, compile a list of topics to search for (you might use standard keyword research to augment this): generally your brand, your competition, your products, and industry-specific topics. Then, conduct the searches and save the results. In many cases, you can set up alerts so that you are notified right away when a conversation is taking place.

You have many options for this process—from completely manual (and free) to engaging an expensive service that not only conducts the searches, but analyzes the information and creates reports on it.

Below are some suggestions on where to start when embarking on this task manually.

- **Use Google search**—With Google advanced options, you can restrict searches to a specific timeframe (such as the last 24 hours) and can even search through only reviews or only discussion forums. You can also use Google Blog Search to search through only blogs and Google News to search through only news (see Figure 9.3).
- **Use Google Alerts**—Google Alerts enables you to set up automated searches for news, blogs, video, groups, and Web search and have the results delivered via e-mail or RSS as they happen, once a day, or once a week.
- **Use vertical search engines**—Take advantage of the search built into many sites. Twitter, YouTube, and Flickr, for instance,

Figure 9.3   Google Search Results: [Taryn Rose]

Source: Google Search Results

all have fairly robust search capabilities. Some sites even let you subscribe to results so you can be alerted to new discussions as they happen.

- **Seek out reviews**—If you sell a product or service, chances are good that someone, somewhere, is reviewing what you have to offer. If you provide a product, check out e-commerce sites, such as Amazon, that encourage reviews. And look for targeted review sites (such as TripAdvisor for travel and Epinions for everything else).
- **Find targeted communities**—Nearly every topic has an enthusiast community and many brands do as well (see Figure 9.4).

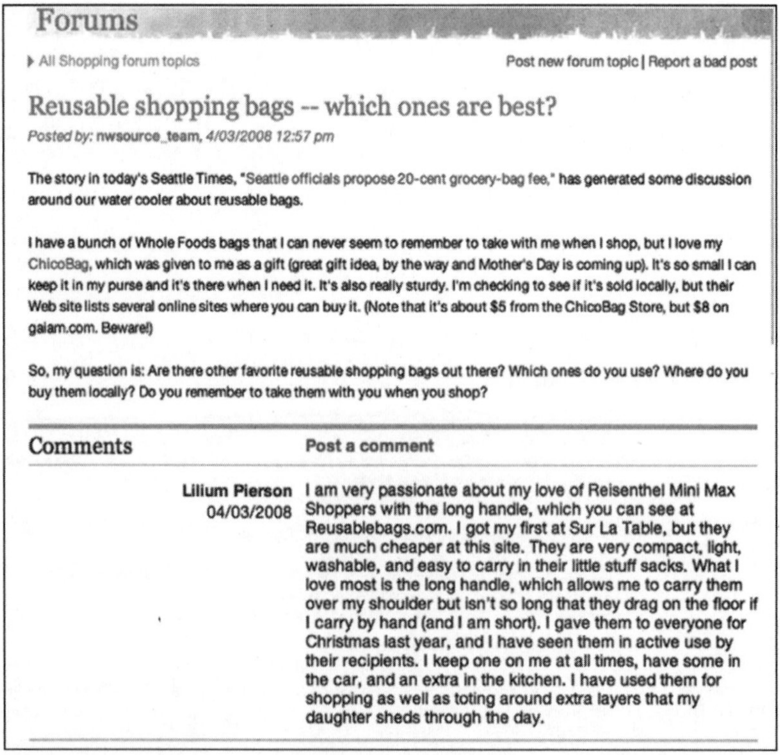

Forums

▸ All Shopping forum topics

Post new forum topic | Report a bad post

Reusable shopping bags -- which ones are best?

Posted by: nwsource_team, *4/03/2008 12:57 pm*

The story in today's Seattle Times, "Seattle officials propose 20-cent grocery-bag fee," has generated some discussion around our water cooler about reusable bags.

I have a bunch of Whole Foods bags that I can never seem to remember to take with me when I shop, but I love my ChicoBag, which was given to me as a gift (great gift idea, by the way and Mother's Day is coming up). It's so small I can keep it in my purse and it's there when I need it. It's also really sturdy. I'm checking to see if it's sold locally, but their Web site lists several online sites where you can buy it. (Note that it's about $5 from the ChicoBag Store, but $8 on galam.com. Beware!)

So, my question is: Are there other favorite reusable shopping bags out there? Which ones do you use? Where do you buy them locally? Do you remember to take them with you when you shop?

Comments

Post a comment

Lilium Pierson 04/03/2008

I am very passionate about my love of Reisenthel Mini Max Shoppers with the long handle, which you can see at Reusablebags.com. I got my first at Sur La Table, but they are much cheaper at this site. They are very compact, light, washable, and easy to carry in their little stuff sacks. What I love most is the long handle, which allows me to carry them over my shoulder but isn't so long that they drag on the floor if I carry by hand (and I am short). I gave them to everyone for Christmas last year, and I have seen them in active use by their recipients. I keep one on me at all times, have some in the car, and an extra in the kitchen. I have used them for shopping as well as toting around extra layers that my daughter sheds through the day.

Figure 9.4 A Community For Every Passion

Source: Screenshot

Figure 9.5   Photo Communities

Source: Flickr

Check Flickr, for instance, for groups, discussions, and photos (see Figure 9.5).

Averting a Public Relations Disaster

Up to the minute focus groups via search of social media chatter don't only provide long-term insight into future product direction and customer engagement, they can alert you to an issue before it becomes a crisis.

When Motrin launched its "baby wearing" campaign, they didn't need to commission a customer survey to find out how viewers perceived it. They had to look no farther than Twitter, a micro blogging service that enables anyone to post short thoughts on the Web (see Figure 9.6).

A quick search the day after the campaign launched revealed that many moms were offended by the campaign, and in fact created the #motrinmom hashtag (a grassroots categorization system that enables users to cluster their posts together under a single topic) to compile their grievances. The negative posts rose quickly (see Figure 9.7).[4]

The *New York Times* noted that within hours of the campaign launch, #motrinmom was the most tweeted subject on Twitter.[5] A YouTube video sprung up that showcased the posts (see Figure 9.8).[6]

Motrin may have had a misstep with the campaign, but they had instant access to amazing consumer feedback. Did they take advantage

Figure 9.6   Motrin Ad: "Baby Wearing"

Source: Motrin

of it? Not at first. In fact, Motrin didn't appear to even realize their customers were talking about them online until a blogger called their agency to ask about the uproar. Once alerted, they took down the ad and said that they "take feedback seriously." And, after the incident, I imagine they are doing a better job of understanding where they might find that feedback in our online world.

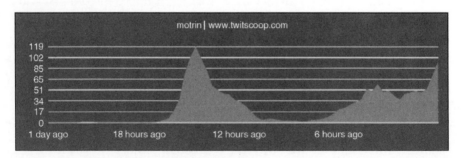

Figure 9.7   [Motrin] Trends on Twitter

Source: Twitscoope.com

Figure 9.8 Mom's Take Their Motrin Anger To YouTube
Source: YouTube.com

But We Want to Control Our Branding!

Many companies are understandably hesitant to enter the new world of social media. After all, historically, only those with media and PR training made official statements on behalf of companies for good reason—an entire brand can be at risk with one wrong comment. And legal and marketing departments the world over have spent substantial resources developing branding guidelines and messaging requirements.

But the truth is that the world has changed. And not participating in the conversation is a loud statement of its own to your customer base. You can't control your branding message in any case because your customers are already talking about you online. The best you can do is to participate.

And the advantages of search alone (through increased visibility in search results and up-to-the-minute market research) make entering this space worthwhile, not to mention the added benefits of better engaging with customers, providing an efficient customer support mechanism, and opening a whole new acquisition channel. (Those latter topics of course, are excellent material for another book.)

But it's smart to be wary of jumping into social media. You want to go about it in the right way, and since you're engaging directly with consumers, you don't want to abandon your efforts halfway through to rethink your strategy.

Here are a few options for getting started:

- **Start with market research.** Find out where your customers and potential customers are talking about you, your competitors, and your industry online and just listen for a while. Gather up the information and get a sense of the overall perception, how your competition is getting involved, what your customers need the most, and what data is most valuable. This alone can provide great insight into your business.
- **Train your PR and marketing staff on social media.** They already have media and PR training and have experience speaking publicly on behalf of the company. They can combine these skills with an understanding of how social media communities work, the importance of authenticity online, and how to respond online.
- **Train your customer support staff on PR and marketing.** Your customer support team already is skilled in dealing with customers (particularly the unhappy ones) one-on-one. You can extend these skills by training them in how to speak publicly on behalf of the company so they can begin treating questions posed on social media sites in a similar way as those posed to them directly over phone or e-mail.
- **Start a blog.** A blog is a great way to start a conversation with your customers. You can use the market research about how your customers are talking about your industry to identify a list of topics to talk about. See a discussion speculating on the next edition of your two-door coupe? Interview the engineer who designed the new dashboard and add a few pictures. Read a blogger's post

questioning the safety record of your competition. Take the initiative and post your own safety record, with backup documentation. In this way, you can begin engaging the community, but at a much smaller scale and with much greater oversight than if you let every employee post on behalf of the company on any social media site they happened upon. Open comments to the blog to evolve this conversation and give a select group of employees the ability to gain experience replying directly online.

- **Create a set of common sense guidelines and let your employees spread the company message.** This suggestion is a scary one, and certainly, it doesn't work for every company. But the truth is that most people are online and it's easy to identify where people work (by virtue of their social networking affiliations, blog bio, or random conversations). Create a set of guidelines about what kind of information not to discuss publicly (such as financial details and upcoming launches), how to speak on behalf of the company (don't promise things on behalf of another department, don't belittle customers), and what's within bounds (offering to pass on feedback, answering questions ("that purse also comes in green and in a larger laptop style")). Since you've hired smart and capable employees who already likely serve as brand ambassadors for you to their friends and family, trust them to do so at a larger scale.

Tactical Suggestions

- Find out where your industry is being discussed to get insight into what potential customers are most interested in.
- Answer questions honestly and provide solutions to problems when you can.
- Provide "inside information" to enthusiasts on blogs or forums.
- When issuing press releases or other resources to bloggers, reporters, or others, ensure you include a URL in addition to a link, link directly to what you are highlighting (not just the home page), and use language that you would like to receive as anchor text.

Figure 9.9   Twitter Search Results: [Obama from: terrymoran]
Source: Twitter.com

- Consider adding a company blog so that you have a convenient source to link back to where you can provide more detailed information.
- If you do add a blog, ensure it's located on your main company domain (at blog.mydomain.com or mydomain.com/blog, for instance) and that it uses backend infrastructure, such as WordPress, that makes it easy to implement search-friendly technical components.
- Understand that posting online is the same as giving an interview to the *New York Times.* And that once it's out there, you can't take it back. This is all common sense stuff. If you're out at dinner with your spouse and mention that you're about to take your company public, someone at the next table might be a reporter who then could write it up as front page news. The difference is that when you post online, *everyone* is at the next table and you can't say that you were misquoted. Consider the ABC reporter who posted an (alleged) off-the-record remark made by President Obama about the recent MTV Video Music Awards. The reporter deleted the comment soon after, but it lives on forever in searches and screenshots (see Figure 9.9).

And deleting comments after the fact can start to look like a cover up and only make matters worse (see Figure 9.10).

Figure 9.10   You Can't Delete Social Media Interaction
Source: Twitter.com

You don't have to go any further than TripAdvisor to find examples of what works and what doesn't. Being apologetic and intent on fixing issues might make potential customers feel as though you care and are appreciative for the feedback (see Figure 9.11).

Being defensive just makes you sound like a jerk (see Figure 9.12).

> **Management Response**
> **NativoLodgeMGMT, Marcos Urtiaga, Front Office Manager**
> (Management representative)
> *Sep 24, 2008*
> We sincerely apologize about your second stay with us and we are concerened that we did not meet the same expectations that we did your first stay with us. The issues that you have addresses have been reported to the management team and we are working on the best solution to prevent them from happening again. Once again, we apologize and hope that we can get another chance to make your stay at the Nativo Lodge as enjoyable as the first.

Figure 9.11   Addressing Consumer Issues Online
Source: Tripadvisor.com

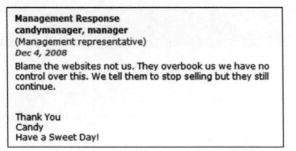

Management Response
candymanager, manager
(Management representative)
Dec 4, 2008
Blame the websites not us. They overbook us we have no
control over this. We tell them to stop selling but they still
continue.

Thank You
Candy
Have a Sweet Day!

Figure 9.12   How Not to Address Consumer Issues Online

Source: Tripadvisor.com

The Value of User-Generated Content for Search Acquisition

User-generated content—that content that you let visitors add to your
site—can be valuable in a number of ways. It helps you have deeper
engagement with your customers (they feel a sense of ownership towards
your brand) and you can more quickly build out content that helps visitors and provides more opportunities to rank in search engines.

But user-generated content is also a lot of work. You need to
engage vocal users early and get them excited about the site. You need to
give users a compelling reason to contribute. And you need to seed the
site with content so that you don't launch empty. You also need internal
oversight—someone to keep things moving along, making sure it's all
headed the right direction.

You Can Compel Visitors by Being Compelling

You need to compel users to spend time on your site and the only way to
do that is to be compelling. How you do that depends on the type of site
that you have. Think about (or talk with your users about) what it is you
have that no one else does. Why do visitors need to come to your site
rather than anyone else's? If you can't come up with anything, then you
may need to work on your site a little before sending out the party invites.

Once you have some value to your site, you need to seed the content a bit before asking others to contribute. You can partner with other

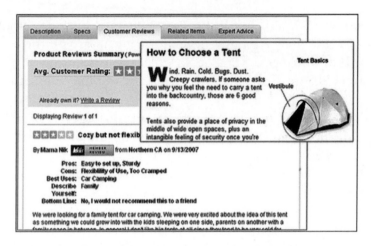

Figure 9.13   Combining Expert and User-Generated Content

Source: Rei.com

content sites (for instance, review sites) to get this content. Just keep in mind that this puts you back into the non-unique content space and those pages are unlikely to rank in search engines. They still may be valuable for seeding purposes though, so you may find that they're still valuable for your needs. Or perhaps you can create a mash up of content that adds unique value on top of each separate component. You can also hire writers to write content for you, although in that case, you should consider how to disclose it (if the writing is for something like reviews). One way is REI's model of both expert and user reviews—each on their own tab (see Figure 9.13).

You can also launch with an invite-only test and get a small group to seed the content for you. The difference between launching publicly with no content and launching to a small invite-only group with no content is that the invited group expects that the site will be empty and they'll know that it's their job to start testing things out. They'll much more happily post to empty pages.

How do you go about an invite-only test? Identify the early adopters and influencers in your niche. Often these are bloggers who are fairly easy to find. You can also check out local or topical forums and find those who post early and often. For instance, I live in West Seattle. The West Seattle blog is run by bloggers who are completely engaged with the local community. They know everything, and they blog it all. If I were looking to jump start user-generated content on a Seattle community site, they would be the first ones I would try to get involved. You can find testers like this everywhere: on social networking sites, at conferences, on Wikipedia.

These are your users who are the most knowledgeable so will likely provide the best contributions, who will contribute the most, and who will spread the word about your site to others.

Once you've got a group, pull them in with flattery. Let them know how great they are and how they can help you with the site. Let them have input during the test phase, and encourage them to contribute lots of content. You may want to leave the test phase by asking your early testers to invite others, rather than opening the site up to everyone initially. This may get your testers talking about your site and providing a bit of buzz.

You also want to consider incentives for those who add content. Some sites have been successful with cash (such as discounts on future purchases) but that can encourage spam, so watch that closely. Better incentives can simply be things like reputation points, elite badges for top posters, and moderator positions. People tend to post online for the fame and glory.

Amazon does this with their top reviewers program. And for years, online forums have been rewarding top posters with special titles and icons.

You should also consider your focus. Don't start too big. What's the core to your site? Start there and expand.

You also need internal oversight to keeps things going and ensure quality. You might be able to do this with outside moderators a la Wikipedia. Or you could allow the community to vote on content. Digg, of course, lets users either vote stories up or bury them. You may end up hiring someone internally. What works for you depends on your site.

Amazon does it by letting you rate the reviews of the Buffy DVDs (see Figure 9.14).

You may want to participate in social networking on other sites, blog, comment on other blogs, jump in and get involved in the community. You can get a better dialogue going with users this way, but you have to be willing to let whoever does that for your company have honest voices.

Figure 9.14   Using Ratings and Reviews to Add Value to Pages

Source: Amazon

Before you get all this going, you should definitely set up some goals and ways to measure them, and you should have a backup plan in case the best laid plans don't lead to the eternal spring fountain. You may need to adjust your site's value add, your incentives, or the group you're engaging. The most important question to ask is: Are you building what people need? That's the best way to keep them coming and coming back.

CHAPTER

What's Next?

Beyond Google and 10 Blue Links

We've already seen that search has progressed substantially from the days of text-only. Search engines have started indexing images, video, and Flash. And search results are reflecting the evolution of the Web by displaying news, video, and images. What's next?

Google isn't going away. As we learned in Chapter 3, Google has become a habit for many searchers and it works well enough that searchers don't have reason to switch. These searchers have also come to expect search that works as well as Google everywhere they navigate online, including their in-site search. Even though Amazon is at its core a retail store, not a search engine, Amazon customers expect Amazon search results to be as relevant and useful to them as Google results are.

Our expectation of effective search everywhere will continue to influence new search engines that use input completely differently from Google's text box and that search over entirely different things. These new search engines won't replace Google. Rather, they'll be additional ways we search as part of everyday activities that may not currently involve search. Google itself will likely begin providing some of these non-text search interfaces over time.

New Search Interfaces

What new search interfaces can we expect to see? Some of them exist already. Shazam[1] is an iPhone application that enables the iPhone owner to hold the phone up to a speaker so Shazam can "listen" to music and identify it. The Urbanspoon[2] iPhone application has a slot machine interface. Simply shake the iPhone and the application detects your location and spins up restaurant locations (see Figure 10.1).

Image Search

A 2009 episode of the television show "Better Off Ted," about a research and development company set twenty-five years in the future featured a revolutionary new product. Ted, the R&D manager, explained, "We've been developing a new search engine, and unlike language-based search engines, this face-matching technology uses visual recognition."[3] Rather than type text into a search box, this search engine would enable searchers to scan a person's photo and would show all other photos containing that person.

Figure 10.1   Urbanspoon iPhone Application
Source: Urbanspoon

Image search engine Face.com took issue with the twenty-five years in the future: "What appears to be science fiction to these guys is a mere reality for our Photo Finder users."[4] Currently available for Facebook only, Photo Finder uses tagged photos of a person to find additional untagged photos.[5] Similarly, image search engine Polar Rose uses facial recognition to find photos of people across the web.

With Google Goggles,[6] launched in December 2009, you can take a photo with your mobile phone's camera and Google will attempt to recognize the item in the photo and return relevant search results. For instance, you can take a picture of a landmark, work of art, or product.

Where's the value to organizations? Beyond potential reputation management issues (in the "Better Off Ted" episode, an executive is found to have a secret life as a magician's assistant through the powers of the image search engine), the most obvious application is e-commerce. I may want to find dresses of a particular color or shoes of a particular style.

With Google Images today, for instance, I can search for similar images. If I see a pair of shoes I like, I can click the "find similar images" link below it and see shoes of a similar style, then click from the image to the web site to buy them (see Figure 10.2).

The product search capabilities in Google Goggles have clear implications for companies. If I'm in a store and take a picture of something I'm thinking of buying, but see it listed for a lower price in Google Goggles, I can just order it online via my phone instead (see Figure 10.3).

Google's YouTube video describing the service explains how it can be used for local search as well. You can point your phone at a local business and Google will display the name of that business and enable you to view information about it. Now, when you walk by a restaurant you've never tried, you can simply aim your phone at the restaurant for instant access to reviews.

In Figure 10.4, you can see that you can simply take a photo of a book cover to access information about it, compare prices, and preview it.

Mobile Search

Many companies, including Google, offer mobile applications that enable you to search via voice rather than text, although strictly speaking,

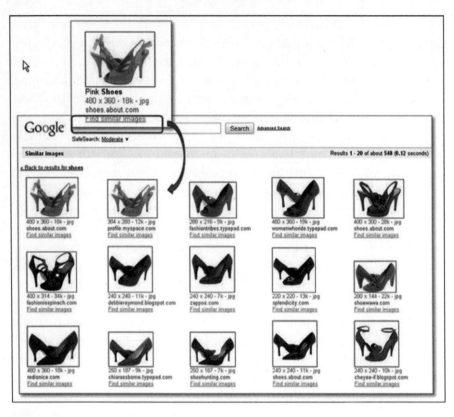

Figure 10.2   Google Similar Images

Source: images.google.com

this type of search is still text-based at its core. It's simply the input mechanism that has changed.

As you saw above with Shazam, Urban Spoon, and Google Goggles, many of the new search interfaces hinge on mobile devices. The ubiquity of mobile devices means we can have search capabilities available wherever we are, for whatever needs we have.

Social Search and Real-Time Search

Social search[7] and real-time search[8] are some of the latest buzzwords to make their way into the search landscape. Both terms have at their core

Figure 10.3   Google Goggles Local Search

Source: YouTube.com

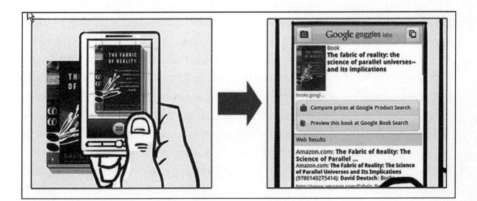

Figure 10.4   Google Goggles Book Search

Source: google.com/mobile/goggles#book

the rise of social networking sites, such as Facebook and Twitter. Initially, the hype was around recommendations from friends. Why search Google and get information from potentially unreliable strangers when you can search your social graph and get advice and recommendations from your personal social circle? So far, that promise remains largely unfulfilled. Turns out, most of us are fairly happy with the reliability of the advice we get on Google, although we may check with our friends (either in person or online) as well.

Now, the search-related value of social networks is focused on real-time information. Search engines such as Google have historically mined the Web and made the content from the Web easy to find. Social networks are creating new content, most of it about things that are happening right now, and then making that searchable. We know that events such as the Super Bowl or an actor's appearance as host on the show *Saturday Night Live* can trigger search spikes. Results on Google for those types of searches will generally provide a broad set of information, including a few listings that are fairly recent (such as news items and content from social networks). But, search on the social networks themselves and you can see in real-time exactly what other people are saying. Think you just felt an earthquake? Grab your cell phone and search Twitter. It's likely you'll find out just where the earthquake was strongest and an initial report of damage before it even hits the news.

The major search engines such as Google have started incorporating real-time search into their results,[9] much as they did a couple of years ago for other types of information, such as images and video.

If Google determines that a particular search query would benefit from results from information being posted in real-time (likely based in part on a search volume spike for that query), then the results may include a "latest results" section that scrolls that information. The latest results section includes content from sources such as Twitter and other microblogging services, Google News, and blogs. For instance, a search for [Justin Bieber] returns not only news, music, images, video, and web pages, but also a section called "Latest results for Justin Bieber" that scrolls Twitter posts from only seconds before (see Figure 10.5).

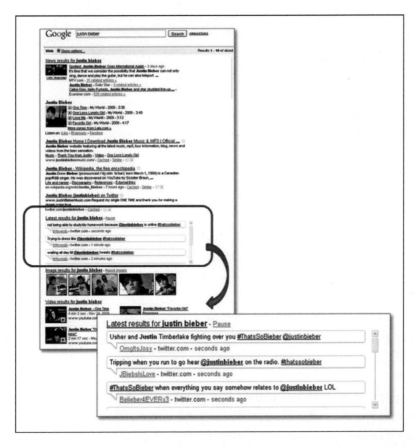

Figure 10.5   Google Real-Time Results

Source: google.com

If you want to search through only real-time results on Google, you can either use the advanced options (choose Show Options, then choose Updates) or you can use the real-time search available through Google Labs.[10] However, as noted earlier, few searchers use advanced options, so most people using Google will only see the real-time results that appear in the "latest results" section of the regular search results (see Figure 10.6).

Microsoft's Bing has taken a somewhat different approach. They have launched a service that enables searchers to see results only from Twitter (and as of this writing, are planning to add Facebook results

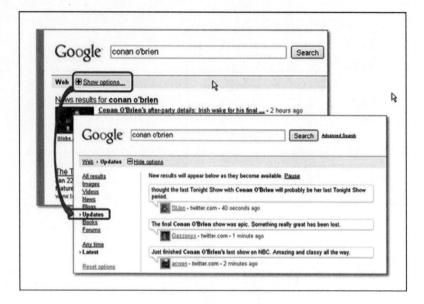

Figure 10.6 Google Updates Option

Source: google.com

as well).[11] For now, searchers have to search directly on this service to see real-time results. Bing includes both recent Twitter posts and top shared links on Twitter (see Figure 10.7).

Bing has incorporated other real-time search elements into its results, although it isn't bringing in real-time search results in the same way Google is. For instance, a search for [Vanessa Fox Twitter] returns my Twitter profile and my most recent posts (see Figure 10.8).

What does the rise of social and real-time search mean for companies? Negative discussions about your brand may become more visible, but your involvement in proactively helping customers solve problems may become more visible as well. As discussed in Chapter 9, the most important step is to start paying attention to social media and how your organization might participate. You can learn about customer issues long before they escalate into PR disasters and can address them proactively. You can also get involved in the conversation. Be helpful. Offer useful information. Provide support. By getting involved now, you'll be ready as this type of search evolves.

Figure 10.7 Microsoft Bing Twitter Search

Source: bing.com/twitter

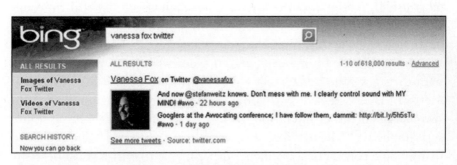

Figure 10.8 Microsoft Bing Twitter Profiles in Web Search

Source: bing.com

Figure 10.9   Google Social Search

Source: google.com

In October 2009, Google rolled out their first attempt at social search as a Google Labs experiment.[12] It shows results from those in your "social circle," initially based on those you subscribe to in Google Reader, your Google Talk and G-mail contacts, and from the social networks you include in your Google Profile (see Figure 10.9).

You can drill into just social search results and see all of your connections who have posted something relevant to your query. You can also see how each person is connected to you (in some cases, they are connected to you through another connection) (see Figure 10.10).

Facebook, of course, provides social search functionality. Want to know what your friends thought of the movie Sherlock Holmes? Just do a quick Facebook search (see Figure 10.11).

Ultimately, the major search engines are looking to provide the most useful, relevant results for searchers. Incorporating real-time and social information is just two of the many ways they are looking to improve how they do this.

In late 2007, a number of search experts and search engine representatives got together to talk about the future of search.[13] Google's Marissa Mayer stressed that Google is balancing the changing needs of searchers and the proliferation of new kinds of content with usability and simplicity. "The paradox of choice is real," she said.[14] She explained that Google continuously launches experiments to only a small percentage of searchers to help guide them toward a better interface rather than simply inundate searchers with choices.

Figure 10.10 Google Social Search Options

Source: google.com

Nearly everyone agreed that a core part of the near future of search was personalization (you can read more about personalization in Chapter 5). Results will become more local for searchers and more tailored to them. Mayer wondered aloud about the value of social search. When you ask friends what good movies they've seen lately, you're explicitly doing a search. How can search engines use that type of behavior to aid better search results? Can you take the social graph and combine it with search? Usability guru Jakob Nielsen chimed in that he felt that social networks were just too small to have positive influence on quality search results. However, as you can see, search engines are experimenting with it, and that's likely to continue.

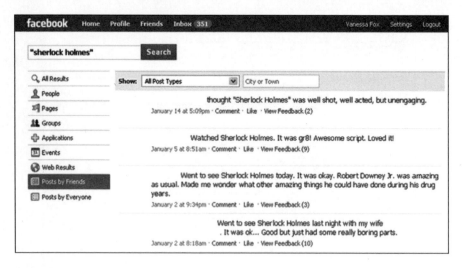

Figure 10.11 Facebook Search

Source: facebook.com

How should companies prepare for the future? The most important step is to realize search isn't going away. Potential customers will continue to research product and company information online, will expect to find customer support there, and will increase online purchasing. Understanding the new customer behavior and buying patterns is vital to the success of any business—from startup to global enterprise, whether an e-commerce site or a business-to-business manufacturer. Media companies, local businesses, and traditional retail brands all can benefit from using search data for customer insights, product development, and business strategy. Organizations should incorporate organic search acquisition strategy into marketing initiatives and Web infrastructure.

Companies that evolve their internal processes and technical frameworks to incorporate organic search and all that it has to offer will have a substantial edge over the competition and will be in an ideal position to take advantage of any new search evolution.

Remember, the customers remain the same—they are simply adapting new behaviors to take advantage of the world of search. You're equipped with the knowledge from this book to adapt with them.

Notes

Preface

1. http://www.google.com/webmasters.

Chapter 1: How Search Has Changed Your Business

1. comscore.com, June 2009.
2. http://www.comscore.com/Press_Events/Press_Releases/2010/1/Global_Search_Market_Grows_46_Percent_in_2009.
3. http://searchengineland.com/can-searchers-find-the-superbowl-16396 (accessed February 2009).
4. http://www.comscore.com/Press_Events/Press_Releases/2010/1/Global_Search_Market_Grows_46_Percent_in_2009.
5. Enquisite Performance Suite™. www.enquisite.com.
6. Author interview with Steven Levy of *Wired* magazine (accessed August 2009).
7. www.cim.co.uk.
8. http://blog.comscore.com/2009/07/print_newspapers_decline.html.
9. A 2007 Web Visible/Nielson study found that 74 percent of respondents used search engines to find local business information versus 65 percent who turned to print Yellow Pages, 50 percent who used Internet Yellow Pages, and 44 percent who used traditional newspapers. AOL Walletpop (http://www.walletpop.com/specials/top-25-things-vanishing-from-america) called the Yellow Pages one of 25 things that were going extinct, along with outhouses and ham radios.

10. eMarketer 2007: 85 percent of online shoppers are also online buyers.

JupiterResearch 2007: U.S. online retail sales will grow by 16 percent in 2007 to reach a total of $116 billion. Over the next five years, U.S. online retail sales will reach $171 billion.

ThirdAge Inc. and JWT Boom 2007: Adults aged 45 years or more likely to shop online. 73 percent of survey respondents indicate shopping is their top online activity.

11. http://www.comscore.com (accessed October 2008).

12. http://www.census.gov/mrts/www/data/pdf/08Q4.pdf (accessed February 2009).

13. http://searchengineland.com/live-blogging-microsoft-searchification-day-2007-12283 (accessed September 2007).

14. http://www.comscore.com/Press_Events/Press_Releases/2007/07/Yahoo!_and_comscore_Online_Consumer_Study (accessed July 2007).

15. http://ir.comscore.com/releasedetail.cfm?ReleaseID=245287 (accessed March 2006).

16. Consumer electronics, toys and hobbies, video games and consoles, and music, movies, and videos enjoy more than 80 percent of conversions from online searches that take place offline.

17. http://www.mediapost.com/publications/?art_aid=99952&fa=Articles.showArticle (accessed February 2009).

18. http://www.enquiroresearch.com/images/Eyetracking2-Sample.pdf (accessed June 2005).

19. Hitwise (accessed May 2009).

20. http://blog.comscore.com/2009/05/longer_search_queries_driving.html (accessed May 2009).

21. eMarketer studies found that 66 percent of searchers distrust paid ads and 29 percent are annoyed by them. iProspect study found that 72 percent of Google searchers feel that organic results are more relevant to their queries than paid ones.

22. http://www.comscore.com.

23. http://papers.ssrn.com/sol3/papers.cfm?abstract_id=1491315 (accessed October 2009).

24. http://www.icrossing.com/articles/Search%20Synergy%20Report.pdf (accessed March 2007).

25. http://pages.enquiro.com/whitepaper-the-brand-lift-of-search.html (accessed May 2009).
26. June 2008, Jupiter Research http://news.cnet.com/8301-1023_3-9980927-93.html.
27. SEMPO Research, www.slideshare.net/massimoburgio/massimo-burgio-sempo-survey-smx-madrid-2008 (accessed May 2008).
28. Michelle Goldberg, a partner at venture capital firm Ignition Partners (accessed September 2009).
29. Nielson.   http://blog.nielsen.com/nielsenwire/online_mobile/multitasking-at-home-simultaneous-use-of-media-grows (accessed September 2009).
30. 2007 iProspect/Jupiter Research study, http://www.iprospect.com/about/researchstudy_2007_offlinechannelinfluence.htm.
31. http://google.com/trends/hottrends?sa=X&date=2009-2-1 (accessed February 2009).
32. http://searchengineland.com/taking-on-arf-engagement-interruptive-advertising-and-whatever-else-youve-got-12598 (accessed November 2007).
33. http://www.useit.com/alertbox/banner-blindness.html (accessed August 2007).
34. http://sethgodin.com/sg/books.asp.
35. http://searchengineland.com/danny-sullivans-ad-age-column-fast-company-debate-10643 (accessed May 2007).
36. http://blog.comscore.com/2009/09/the_revenge_of_neglected_brand.html (accessed September 2009).
37. Author interview with Conrad Saam, Vice President of Marketing for Avvo (accessed January 2010).

Chapter 2: How to Use Search Data to Improve Your Business and Product Strategy

1. Fourteen percent of searches are followed by a second, more specific search (called a refinement) and 24 percent result in a quick click back from the chosen site to the search results. Twenty-one percent of search sessions are longer than 10 minutes (accessed Microsoft internal slides) (accessed June 2009).

2. http://www.hitwise.com/us/press-center/press-releases/google-searches-sept-09 (accessed September 2009).

3. Miller, Geoffrey. 2009. *Spent: Sex, Evolution, and Consumer Behavior.* New York: Viking Adult.

4. Honomichl Annual Industry Report (Jack Honomichl and Laurence N. Gold), 2007.

5. For more on these testing methods, see *Call to Action: Secret Formulas to Improve Online Results,* by Bryan and Jeffrey Eisenberg and *Landing Page Optimization* by Tim Ash.

6. Google AdWords Keyword Tool, September 2009.

7. http://googleresearch.blogspot.com/2009/08/on-predictability-of-search-trends.html (accessed August 2009).

8. http://research.google.com/archive/google_trends_predictability .pdf.

9. http://google.com/insights/search.

10. http://google.com/googleblogs/pdfs/google_predicting_the_present .pdf.

11. http://www.washingtonpost.com/wp-dyn/content/article/2009/09/11/AR2009091103771.html (accessed September 2009).

12. https://adwords.google.com/select/KeywordToolExternal.

13. http://labs.wordtracker.com/keyword-questions.

14. http://compete.com.

15. http://spyfu.com.

16. http://trends.google.com/websites.

17. http://www.alexa.com.

18. http://www.hitwise.com.

19. http://www.comscore.com.

20. http://en-us.nielsen.com/tab/product_families/nielsen_netratings.

Chapter 3: How We Search

1. http://www.hitwise.com/us/press-center/press-releases/google-searches-sept-09 (accessed September 2009).

2. http://www.seobythesea.com/?p=1021.

3. http://en.wikipedia.org/wiki/Bounded_rationality.

4. http://live.psu.edu/story/40091.

5. http://weblogs.hitwise.com/us-heather-hopkins/2009/08/only_70_ of_canadian_searches_a.html (accessed August 2009).
6. http://www.iprospect.com/premiumPDFs/WhitePaper_2006_Search EngineUserBehavior.pdf (accessed April 2006).
7. David Robins research, Louisiana State University.
8. http://www.amazon.com/Why-We-Buy-Science-Shopping/dp/068 4849143.
9. http://searchengineland.com/human-hardware-men-and-women-13 614 (accessed May 2008).
10. http://www.searchengineguide.com/gord-hotchkiss/inside-the-mind- of-the-searcher-part-ii-search-behavior-explored.php (accessed June 2004).
11. Researcher Wendy Wood research, Duke University.
12. http://www.outofmygord.com/archive/2009/01/21/A-Cognitive- Walk-Through-of-Searching.aspx (accessed January 2009).
13. http://en.wikipedia.org/wiki/The_Magical_Number_Seven,_Plus_ or_Minus_Two.
14. http://www-news.ucdavis.edu/search/news_detail.lasso?id=8592 (accessed April 2008).
15. http://searchengineland.com/human-hardware-searching-with-the- basal-ganglia-14578 (accessed August 2008).
16. Enquiro.
17. http://www.iprospect.com/premiumPDFs/WhitePaper_2006_Search EngineUserBehavior.pdf (accessed April 2006).
18. http://www.jimboykin.com/click-rate-for-top-10-search-results (accessed August 2006).
19. http://ist.psu.edu/faculty_pages/jjansen.
20. http://searchengineland.com/yahoo-searchmonkey-enhanced-listings- available-to-searchers-14150 (accessed June 2008).
21. Lindgaard, G., Dudek, C., Fernandes, G., and Brown, J. (accessed 2006) "Attention web designers: You have 50 milliseconds to make a good first impression!" *Behaviour & Information Technology 25*: 115-126.
22. Underhill, Paco. 2000. *Why We Buy: The Science of Shopping*. New York: Simon & Schuster.
23. For more comprehensive information about Web site usability and Web site optimization, refer to *Don't Make Me Think: A Common*

Sense Approach to Web Usability by Steve Krug and to Jakob Nielsen's work. http://www.useit.com.

Chapter 4: Building Searcher Personas

1. Persona definition courtesy of Tamara Adlin, author of *The Essential Persona Lifecycle: Your Guide to Building and Using Personas.*
2. Read *The Essential Persona Lifecycle: Your Guide to Building and Using Personas* to learn more about prioritizing personas based on their business value.
3. http://en.wikipedia.org/wiki/The_Long_Tail.
4. Hitwise, September 2008.
5. http://www.slideshare.net/studentlamarketing/enquiro-white-paper-the-brand-lift-of-search (accessed 2007).
6. http://www.iprospect.com/premiumPDFs/WhitePaper_2006_SearchEngineUserBehavior.pdf (accessed April 2006).
7. http://googleblog.blogspot.com/2009/10/managing-your-reputation-through-search.html (accessed October 2009).
8. http://www.flickr.com/photos/windo/3948998275.

Chapter 5: How Search Engines Work

1. http://www.google.com/intl/en/corporate/tech.html.
2. Yahoo! began in the mid-1990s as a manual directory and transitioned into an automated search engine. Google launched in 1998. Microsoft launched a search engine of its own in 2004 (it previously licensed technology from other companies).
3. http://searchengineland.com/microsoft-yahoo-search-deal-simplified-23299 (accessed July 2009).
4. http://googleblog.blogspot.com/2008/05/introduction-to-google-search-quality.html (accessed May 2008).
5. http://searchengineland.com/jakob-nielsen-on-search-usability-11688 (accessed July 2007).
6. http://www.google.com/support/accounts/bin/topic.py?topic=14148.
7. http://searchengineland.com/just-behave-googles-marissa-mayer-on-personalized-search-10592 (accessed February 2007).

8. http://searchengineland.com/googles-matt-cutts-on-personalization-and-the-future-of-seo-10649 (accessed May 2007).
9. http://searchengineland.com/googles-personalized-results-the-new-normal-31290.
10. http://googlewebmastercentral.blogspot.com/2007/05/taking-advantage-of-universal-search.html (accessed May 2007).
11. http://searchengineland.com/qa-with-marissa-mayer-google-vp-search-products-user-experience-10370 (accessed January 2007).
12. comscore.com (accessed October 2008).
13. http://searchengineland.com/up-close-google-squared-19313.
14. http://searchengineland.com/google-adds-more-answers-info-to-search-results-34221.
15. http://searchengineland.com/get-youtube-videos-in-your-google-product-search-feeds-25576 (accessed September 2009).
16. http://blog.nielsen.com/nielsenwire/online_mobile/total-online-video-streams-up-41-from-last-year (accessed September 2009).
17. comscore (accessed October 2008).
18. http://www.comscore.com/Press_Events/Press_Releases/2009/10/TV_Season_Premieres_Spur_Continued_Gains_in_Online_Video_Viewing_as_September_Attracts_Record_Viewership.
19. http://searchengineland.com/eye-tracking-on-universal-and-personalized-search-12233 (accessed September 2007).
20. Progressive enhancement is a way of building Web pages that layers technology elements so that a visitor using any browser type (even those that don't support the latest technologies) can access the basic content.
21. http://searchengineland.com/the-google-quality-raters-handbook-13575 (accessed May 2008).
22. http://www.w3.org/WAI.

Chapter 6: Implementing an Effective Search Strategy

1. http://www.searchmarketingexpo.com.
2. Seattle Tech Startup Mailing List (accessed August 2009).
3. Alex Bosworth, http://www.ninebyblue.com/blog/seo-is-the-worst-thing-ever-invented (accessed March 2008).
4. Jeremy Schoemaker, http://www.shoemoney.com.

5. http://powazek.com/posts/2090 (accessed October 2009).
6. http://www.foxnews.com/slideshow/scitech/2009/08/17/marketing-internet-scams?slide=6 (accessed August 2008).
7. http://www.google.com/support/webmasters/bin/answer.py?answer=35769.
8. http://en.wikipedia.org/wiki/Meta_element#The_keywords_attribute.
9. *Call to Action: Secret Formulas for Improve Online Results* by Bryan and Jeffrey Eisenberg for more on this topic.
10. Anchor texts are the words used to describe the link.
11. http://www.google.com/support/webmasters/bin/answer.py?answer=35291.

Chapter 7: Working with Developers

1. http://sitemaps.org.
2. http://googlewebmastercentral.blogspot.com/2008/11/date-with-googlebot-part-ii-http-status.html (accessed November 2008).
3. http://www.google.com/webmasters.
4. http://janeandrobot.com/library/managing-robots-access-to-your-website (accessed December 2008).
5. http://googlewebmastercentral.blogspot.com/2008/11/date-with-googlebot-part-ii-http-status.html (accessed November 2008).
6. http://janeandrobot.com/library/managing-robots-access-to-your-website (accessed December 2008).
7. http://searchengineland.com/canonical-tag-16537 (accessed February 2009).
8. http://searchengineland.com/google-lets-you-tell-them-which-url-parameters-to-ignore-25925 (accessed September 2009).
9. http://janeandrobot.com/library/domain-canonicalization (accessed May 2009).
10. http://searchengineland.com/canonical-tag-16537 (accessed February 2009).
11. http://searchengineland.com/google-lets-you-tell-them-which-url-parameters-to-ignore-25925 (accessed September 2009).
12. http://janeandrobot.com/library/managing-robots-access-to-your-website (accessed December 2008).

13. http://googlewebmastercentral.blogspot.com/2008/10/first-click-free-for-web-search.html.
14. http://janeandrobot.com/library/effectively-using-images (accessed May 2008).
15. http://www.comscore.com/Press_Events/Press_releases/2009/9/comscore_Releases_August_2009_U.S._Search_Engine_Rankings (accessed September 2009).
16. http://googlevideo.blogspot.com/2008/05/video-sitemaps-how-we-find-great-videos.html (accessed May 2008).
17. http://googlewebmastercentral.blogspot.com/2007/09/improve-snippets-with-meta-description.html (accessed September 2007).

Chapter 8: How to Cut through Data and Get the Actionable Metrics You Need

1. http://www.techcrunch.com/2009/07/09/the-naked-truth-2009-slides-show-me-the-money (accessed July 2009).
2. Kaushik, Avinash. 2007. *Web Analytics: An Hour a Day*. New York: Sybex.
3. http://www.kaushik.net/avinash/2006/07/stop-obsessing-about-conversion-rate.html (accessed July 2006).
4. http://webanalyticssolutionprofiler.com.
5. http://ir.comscore.com/releasedetail.cfm?ReleaseID=245287 (accessed March 2006).
6. http://www.comscore.com/Press_Events/Press_Releases/2008/01/Importance_of_Search_Engines (accessed January 2008).
7. http://www.doubleclick.com/insight/pdfs/searchpurchase_0502.pdf (accessed February 2005).
8. Author interview with Greg Fant (August 2009).
9. http://www.enquisite.com.
10. http://www.clearsaleing.com/wp-content/uploads/2009/07/am-buyers-guide-handout-final.pdf (accessed July 2009).
11. http://www.attributionmanagement.com/2009/10/attribution-management-buyers-guide-part-2-and-3 (accessed October 2009).
12. http://www.iprospect.com/premiumPDFs/researchstudy_2007_offlinechannelinfluence.pdf (accessed August 2007).

13. http://www.emarketer.com/Article.aspx?R=1005971 (accessed February 2008).
14. http://searchengineland.com/attributing-value-to-phone-calls-dynamic-number-insertion-can-help-26339 (accessed September 2009).
15. http://www.kaushik.net/avinash/2006/06/data-quality-sucks-lets-just-get-over-it.html (accessed June 2006).

Chapter 9: Social Media and Search

1. For a more comprehensive discussion of social media strategy, see *Friends with Benefits: A Social Media Marketing Handbook* by Darren Barefoot and Julie Szabo.
2. Google AdWords Keyword Tool, average global monthly search volume (accessed September 2009).
3. Google AdWords Keyword Tool, average global monthly search volume (accessed September 2009).
4. http://www.marketingpilgrim.com/2008/11/motrin-faces-twitter-headache-over-new-video-campaign.html (accessed November 2008).
5. http://parenting.blogs.nytimes.com/2008/11/17/moms-and-motrin (accessed November 2008).
6. http://www.youtube.com/watch?v=LhR-y1N6R8Q (accessed November 2008).

Chapter 10: What's Next?

1. http://www.shazam.com/music/web/pages/iphone.html.
2. http://www.urbanspoon.com/blog/27/Urbanspoon-on-the-iPhone.html (accessed July 2008).
3. http://abc.go.com/watch/better-off-ted/187472/228393/secrets-and-lives.
4. http://blog.face.com/2009/08/20/better-off-ted.
5. http://blog.face.com/2009/03/24/photofinderlaunch.
6. http://searchengineland.com/google-goggles-search-by-images-31364.
7. http://searchengineland.com/the-impending-social-search-inflection-point-10885 (accessed April 2007).

8. http://searchengineland.com/what-is-real-time-search-definitions-players-22172 (accessed July 2009).
9. http://searchengineland.com/search-in-the-year-2010-11917 (accessed August 2007).
10. http://searchengineland.com/google-launches-real-time-search-31355.
11. http://www.google.com/webhp?esrch=RTSearch.
12. http://searchengineland.com/live-today-bings-twitter-search-engine-28224.
13. http://searchengineland.com/google-social-search-launches-gives-results-from-your-trusted-social-circle-28507.
14. See *The Paradox of Choice: Why More Is Less* by Barry Schwartz.

References

Adlin, Tamara, and John Pruitt. (2006). *The Persona Lifecycle: Keeping People in Mind Throughout Product Design (The Morgan Kaufmann Series in Interactive Technologies)*. San Francisco: Morgan Kaufmann.

Albert, William, and Thomas Tullis. (2008). *Measuring the User Experience: Collecting, Analyzing, and Presenting Usability Metrics (Interactive Technologies)*. San Francisco: Morgan Kaufmann.

Ash, Tim. (2008). *Landing Page Optimization*. Hoboken, NJ: John Wiley & Sons, Inc.

Barefoot, Darren, and Julie Szabo. (2009). *Friends with Benefits: Online Marketing with Blogs, Facebook, YouTube, and More*. San Francisco: No Starch Press.

Berkman, Robert. (2008). *The Art of Strategic Listening: Finding Market Intelligence in Blogs and Social Media*. Ithaca, NY: Paramount Market Publishing, Inc.

Clifton, Brian. (2008). *Advanced Web Metrics with Google Analytics*. New York: Sybex.

Eisenberg, Bryan, Jeffrey Eisenberg, and Lisa T. Davis. (2006). *Call to Action: Secret Formulas to Improve Online Results*. Nashville, Tennessee: Nelson Business.

Enge, Eric, Stephen Spencer, Rand Fishkin, and Jessie Stricchiola. (2009). *The Art of SEO (Theory in Practice)*. Sebastopol, CA: O'Reilly Media.

Godin, Seth. (1999). *Permission Marketing: Turning Strangers Into Friends And Friends Into Customers*. New York: Simon & Schuster.

Hunt, Bill, and Mike Moran. (2008). *Search Engine Marketing, Inc.: Driving Search Traffic to Your Company's Web Site* (2nd Edition). New York: IBM Press.

Kaushik, Avinash. (2007). *Web Analytics: An Hour a Day*. New York: Sybex.

Kaushik, Avinash. (2009). *Web Analytics 2.0: The Art of Online Accountability and Science of Customer Centricity*. New York: Sybex.

Krug, Steve. (2005). *Don't Make Me Think: A Common Sense Approach to Web Usability* (2nd Edition). Berkeley, CA: New Riders Press.

Loveday, Lance, and Sandra Niehaus. (2007). *Web Design for ROI: Turning Browsers into Buyers & Prospects into Leads*. Berkeley, CA: New Riders Press.

Schwartz, Barry. (2005). *The Paradox of Choice: Why More Is Less*. New York: Harper Perennial.

Scott, David Meerman. (2008). *The New Rules of Marketing and PR: How to Use News Releases, Blogs, Podcasting, Viral Marketing and Online Media to Reach Buyers Directly*. Hoboken, NJ: John Wiley & Sons, Inc.

Thurow, Shari. (2007). *Search Engine Visibility: Voices that Matter* (2nd Edition). Berkeley, CA: Peachpit Press.

Index